A central political issue in American politics during the 1990s is the need for political campaign reform. A variety of proposals have been advanced to reform the system of congressional elections, most notably in relation to campaign financing. The authors examine U.S. Senate elections to determine the role money plays in the contests; their analysis indicates that the system of campaign finance resembles a market, with legislators serving as the recipients of financial largesse based on their institutional positions and political vulnerability. This rent-seeking relationship between economic interests and legislators has transformed the dynamic of Senate elections.

Assessing the potential impact of several electoral reform proposals, Professors Regens and Gaddie argue that debates over the nature and consequences of proposed changes in election finance are often waged without an underlying point of theoretical reference. In addition, little consideration is placed upon impacts relative to each other or collectively on the political system. Spending limits and public funding proposals, they contend, will not have the effects expected by reform advocates. Term limit and public funding proposals would disrupt the rent-seeking relationship between legislators and economic interests, and these proposals would also face political and constitutional barriers to implementation.

The economic realities of political reform

Murphy Institute Studies in Political Economy
General Editor: Richard F. Teichgraeber III

The books in the series are occasional volumes sponsored by the
Murphy Institute of Political Economy at Tulane University and
Cambridge University Press, comprising original essays by lead-
ing scholars in the United States and other countries. Each volume considers one of the intellectual preoccupations or analytical
preoccupations or analytical procedures currently associated with
the term "political economy." The goal of the series is to aid
scholars and teachers committed to moving beyond the traditional
boundaries of their disciplines in a common search for new insights
and new ways of studying the political and economic realities of
our time. The series is published with the support of the Tulane-
Murphy Foundation.

Also in the series:
Gordon C. Winston and Richard F. Teichgraeber III, eds.,
    The boundaries of economics
John Dunn, ed., *The economic limits to modern politics*
Thomas L. Haskell and Richard F. Teichgraeber III, eds.,
    The culture of the market: Historical essays

The economic realities of political reform

Elections and the U. S. Senate

James L. Regens
Tulane University

Ronald Keith Gaddie
Tulane University

CAMBRIDGE UNIVERSITY PRESS

CAMBRIDGE UNIVERSITY PRESS
Cambridge, New York, Melbourne, Madrid, Cape Town, Singapore, São Paulo

Cambridge University Press
The Edinburgh Building, Cambridge CB2 2RU, UK

Published in the United States of America by Cambridge University Press, New York

www.cambridge.org
Information on this title: www.cambridge.org/9780521474689

First published 1995
This digitally printed first paperback version 2005

A catalogue record for this publication is available from the British Library

Library of Congress Cataloguing in Publication data

Regens, James L.
    The economic realities of political reform : elections and the
    U. S. Senate / James L. Regens, Ronald Keith Gaddie.
      p. cm. — (Murphy Institute studies in political economy)
    Includes bibliographical references and index.
    ISBN 0–521–47468–X (hardback)
    1. Campaign Funds – United States. 2. United States. Senate –
Elections. 3. Electioneering – United States. 4. Politics,
Practical – United States. I. Gaddie, Ronald Keith. II. Title.
III. Series.
JK1991.R425   1995
324.7′8′0973–dc20   94–30030
                                                CIP

ISBN-13 978-0-521-47468-9 hardback
ISBN-10 0-521-47468-X hardback

ISBN-13 978-0-521-02351-1 paperback
ISBN-10 0-521-02351-3 paperback

Contents

Tables and figures

Tables

Figures

Acknowledgments

Our motivation for writing this book stems from a desire to explore whether the concept of rent seeking/rent provision is a satisfactory paradigm for assessing the role of money in electoral politics. The manuscript is the culmination of an intellectual odyssey through the world of campaign finance and interest groups. The insightful and occasionally heated observations of colleagues, reviewers, and discussants at conferences contributed to crystallizing our own perspectives. We would like to thank Robert Grafstein, Glenn Parker, Brad Lockerbie, Euel Elliott, Michael Munger, Kevin Grier, Scott Ainsworth, Paul Herrnson, Laura Junor, and Chuck Bullock for their comments and criticisms of various papers and manuscripts that preceded this volume. The critical comments and support of Rick Teichgraeber, Director of the Murphy Institute of Political Economy at Tulane University, is also greatly appreciated, as are the constructive criticisms of the reviewers at Cambridge University Press and our editor, Scott Parris. Naturally, we remain responsible for the interpretations offered.

Abbreviations

PAC	Political action committee
FECA	Federal Election Campaign Act
FCPA	Federal Corrupt Practices Act
FEC	Federal Elections Commission
FHLBB	Federal Home Loan Bank Board
LUR	Lowest-unit-rate
CIO-PAC	Congress of Industrial Operators Political Action Committee
OLS	Ordinary least squares

Introduction

In recent years the more prominent face of the Senate has been its individualistic one. The contemporary institution is a collection of entrepreneurs, each one in business for himself or herself, each one with a personal agenda and goals.

Richard F. Fenno
Learning to Legislate: The Senate Education of Arlen Specter

The contemporary debate that surrounds the conduct of congressional elections has its origins in an enduring argument about the importance of money in politics. Among his numerous sage observations about the American political scene, the late Samuel Clemens noted, "Ours is the best Congress money can buy!" Nonetheless, although a burgeoning literature has emerged examining campaign contributions from organized interests, the lack of a robust, theoretical paradigm that accounts for the dynamics of legislator and interest-group interaction in the context of funding elections is troubling. Arguments over the nature and consequences of proposed changes in the approach to financing congressional elections are often waged without an underlying point of theoretical reference. Reform proposals are presented and bandied about with little consideration for their impacts relative to each other, or collectively, on the political system.

This volume seeks to provide a theoretical yardstick for evaluating those proposals. We contend that the behavior of legislators in seeking financial support for their reelection campaigns can be viewed in the same fashion as profit-seeking firms. Senators are members of a highly exclusive legislative body, whose policy imperatives have far-reaching economic and social consequences. Numerous avenues exist for special-interest influence of legislators, and interests use these to extract favorable policy outputs. Many of these avenues afford opportunities for interests to make wealth transfers to legislators, indicating that interests are positioned to provide legislators with "extra pay," or "rents" (Parker, 1992a).

Rent seeking

One of the problems confronting British economists in the early 1800s was the need to explain why landlords earned differential rates of return from their lands, whereas tenants who farmed those lands tended to accrue the same rate of return. The answer to this question is found if we relax the assumption that all inputs of a particular kind are equal, especially when the existence of factors of production with a fixed supply occurs (see Stigler, 1987). In this case, the amount of land available for cultivation may vary in its quality although the quantities of various categories are relatively fixed. Higher quality land would be preferred to lesser quality land, and tenants would compete among themselves to lease the available land. Competition among tenants bid up the price they were willing to pay for access to land to the point at which their average cost equaled their average revenue. This represents the opportunity cost of employment in farming. As a result, the owners of better grades of land commanded higher rates of return because the landlord owned a factor of production that was in absolutely fixed supply. The resulting payment received could exceed the opportunity cost or normal profit of leasing the land. In essence, they might capture a return beyond the minimum necessary to induce willingness to lease. This excess profit, all of which accrued to the landlord, represents an economic rent.[1]

By implication, a reduction of the share of payments allocated to rents will not influence the availability of inputs, whereas a reduction in nonrents is likely to alter resource allocation. To see why, suppose the absolute quantity of some input (in this case, Senators) illustrated in Figure I.1 is fixed at A so its supply curve is vertical. The price of this input is determined entirely by the demand curve and any actual payment above zero exceeds the minimum necessary to attract the supply. All payments received by the owner of any input in fixed supply, therefore, are entirely rents. Some portion of the payments received for inputs with upwardly sloping supply curves also constitute

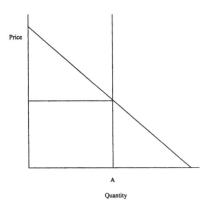

Figure 1.1. *Costs of policy with a vertical supply curve*

economic rents. Consequently, the more inelastic the supply curve, the greater rents are as a proportion of total payments.

In recent years, there has been a tendency by economists to recognize that the concept of rents encompasses all payments for inputs above the minimum necessary to make them available to a firm or to the economy. The similarities between market choice and political choice in a democratic setting are widely recognized (see Downs, 1957). Tullock (1980a, 1980b) demonstrated that resources used in seeking to influence political choices involve potentially contestable transfers among groups or individuals (Becker, 1983; Tollison, 1982). Paul and Wilhite (1990) similarly demonstrate how a variety of political activities from waging war to seeking elective office can be understood as rent-seeking games (Parker, 1992a; Gopoian, 1984)

Traditional rent seeking is derived from regulatory analysis. According to George Stigler (1971), industries can view the outputs of government – in the form of economic regulation – either as threats due to onerous regulation or as benefits that enhance the firms' profits. In the case of acquired benefits, firms seek to obtain regulation from government that serves to benefit the industry by providing subsidies or by restricting entry into the political arena.[2] Tullock (1980b, 1965) sought to more readily define the nature of the profit obtained by industries from beneficial regulation. According to Tullock's ar-

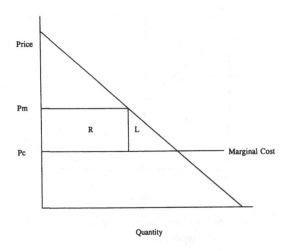

Figure 1.2. *The social costs of monopoly with rent seeking*

gument, under perfect competition an industry will obtain profits based on a price equal to the marginal costs of production of the good or service (see Figure 1.2). However, firms also seek to constrain entry to a market, thereby limiting the level of competition for consumer business (see also Parker, 1992b). By constraining the product market to monopolistic or oligopolistic levels, firms are able to set prices that exceed the marginal cost of production. The area between the curve representing the marginal costs of production (DF) and the monopoly price (BP) and the point of monopoly constrained supply (CE) is the excess profit, or rent, obtained by the firm (square BCDE). Firms pursuing regulation that provides such an excess profit are termed rent seekers. Those who succeed in obtaining such regulation are rent gainers.[3]

This underscores the potential for participants in the political process to attempt to influence the choices made by public officials. Economic models of individual, as well as collective behavior, characteristically assume that such rational self-interest underlies the pursuit of future well-being (see Keech, 1991; Mitchell and Munger, 1991). Self-interest provides an extremely powerful incentive for attempting to realize one's ambitions through concerted political action.

Examples of mutually self-serving behavior by elected officials and regulated interests abound in American political history. In many instances, the activities observed are legal, whereas other examples stretch the limits of credibility and ethical behavior. Lyndon Johnson arrived in Congress during the Great Depression with virtually no money or real property. Johnson spent the rest of his adult years in public office. Nonetheless, when LBJ retired from public life in 1969, his net worth was in excess of $22 million, although he never made more than $50,000 in a year before 1961. Although some wealth was derived from his marriage to the daughter of a Texas merchant, the control and sale of FCC licenses in Texas created much of Johnson's wealth, as did the extensive public works money diverted to improve and develop his LBJ Ranch. In many respects, Lyndon Johnson represented the extreme of an individual's ability to grow wealthy in Congress (Caro, 1982; Miller, 1980).

Several politicians have furthered their political careers through the exercise of influence on behalf of special interests. The Nixon Administration is alleged to have orchestrated the overthrow of the Chilean government in exchange for political support from ITT. A similar example, from the same administration, is the milk price supports offered to dairy producers in exchange for almost $2.5 million in campaign contributions. On a smaller scale, numerous examples abound of individual politicians using their influence on behalf of financial supporters. The most prominent examples of the last decade are the revealed relationship between a cohort of U.S. Senators and a developer and S&L president known as the Keating Five scandal, and the controversy surrounding the involvement of Bill Clinton in the Whitewater Development Project, which was financed by a failed Arkansas S&L.

The Keating Five scandal emerged to public view with the publication by the *Detroit News* of the details surrounding the intervention by Michigan Senator Donald Riegle with federal savings and loan regulators in 1987. Riegle, chairman of the Banking Committee in the Senate, intervened on behalf of the president of Lincoln Savings Bank, Charles Keating, whose thrift was under investigation. Riegle first came into contact with Keating's dilemma through the problems surrounding Keating's Ponchartrain Hotel in Detroit. Riegle, after

meeting with one of Keating's auditors from Lincoln Savings, intervened with Federal Home Loan Banking Board (FHLBB) Chairman
Edwin Gray and told him of the concerns of several western Senators
regarding Keating's treatment by regulators. Riegle and at least one
other Senator asked Gray to back off. Later in 1987, Riegle raised almost $78,000 at a fund raiser held at Keating's Detroit Ponchartrain
Hotel and attended by many Keating associates and friends.

The other four members of the Keating Five had varying degrees
of involvement. Senators Dennis Deconcini and John McCain of Arizona, Alan Cranston (CA), and John Glenn (OH) were also impli-
cated in the plan to place pressure on federal thrift regulators. McCain
and Glenn were only peripherally involved and were found by
the Senate Ethics Committee to have exercised "poor judgement."
McCain had only attended two meetings with regulators and returned
a Keating campaign contribution, whereas John Glenn refused a
Keating offer to hold a $200,000 fund raiser for the debt-straddled
former presidential candidate. Cranston and Deconcini, like Riegle,
did not demonstrate such restraint. Deconcini, considered Keating's
principle advocate with Riegle, accepted $48,000 in Keating contri-
butions. Cranston accepted no personal campaign support, but his
California voter registration project (headed by Cranston's son) received almost $875,000 in Keating money.

Keating's Lincoln Savings and Loan continued in business for almost two years after the intervention with the federal investigation.
The intervention delayed the takeover and closing of Lincoln, which
went bankrupt in 1989. The federal bailout of Keating's S&L may
cost taxpayers over $2 billion, a cost that could have been much lower
(or averted) if regulators had not been pressured by Senators who
were seeking to fund their reelection campaigns. The authors of the
Almanac of American Politics noted that, in the case of Riegle, "it
was money for this [1988 reelection] campaign that linked him with
Charles Keating (Barone and Ujifusa, 1991: 608).

Political resources as rents

One obvious way to seek access, and implicitly gain influence, is
through the provision of politically valuable resources. In fact, orga-

nized interests have long been thought to allocate their monetary and other resources in ways intended to affect political outcomes (see Grier, Munger, and Torrent, 1990). The proliferation of political action committees (PACs) starting in the late 1970s provided interest groups with a convenient way of targeting campaign contributions to candidates.[4] It is plausible that their allocation strategies should be readily observable because the campaign finance process functions as a quasi market for the provision and extraction of rents. Seeking rents in the form of enhanced contributions presumably is rational behavior for ambitious politicians who want to guarantee reelection. Providing differential rents through political campaign contributions, by implication, is similarly rational for the business community, labor, interest groups, and political parties. These entities will then attempt to influence legislators to provide favorable regulation or legislative outcomes, but will do so only to the point that the net advantage obtained through a favorable outcome is not dissipated by the effort (i.e., inefficient rent seeking).

Description of chapters

This study examines the financing of Senate elections in the United States. The rent-seeking paradigm serves as a framework for our examination of senatorial and interest group behavior. By examining the fund-raising behavior of Senators, the financial allocations of economic interests, and the importance of spending in Senate elections, we systematically demonstrate how the behavior of Senate incumbents resembles that of profit-seeking firms in a self-regulated market.

The evolution of the Senate and the campaign-finance regime are discussed in Chapter 1. The changes in the campaign-finance system originate from the same sources as the institutional evolution in the Senate: the needs of members. Based on the assumption that members of a profitable enterprise with limited positions will act to erect entry barriers to protect their own position in the enterprise, we argue that the emergence of an expanded government role in economic regulation, coupled with the rise of interest groups, makes the Congress an attractive place for legislators. The change in campaign finance that created the current PAC regime is discussed. A theory of legislators as rent-seeking firms is presented.

Chapter 2 analyzes trends in fund raising by U.S. Senators. The analyses note two trends indicative of rent-seeking behavior by legislators: the increase in early-term fund raising to create entry barriers and the ability of Senators to run superefficient campaigns with large financial surpluses. Early fund raising by Senators is reflective of the vulnerability of the legislators' policy position. Potentially vulnerable Senators reveal a marked dependence on political PAC support. The ability of Senators to run superefficient campaigns, by comparison, is more common of Senators who are relatively independent of PACs.

In Chapter 3, we examine the contribution strategies of the major economic PACs. Contributions from the four distinct economic PAC cohorts (corporate, labor, trade, and cooperative) are examined to determine the degree to which these PACs' allocation strategies support the rent-seeking-firm hypothesis. Incumbent receipts from these PACs were closely related to institutional and electoral attributes. The allocations by PACs to incumbents indicate that economic interests have sophisticated contribution strategies for targeting financial resources. These strategies not only emphasize rewarding friends, but also result in substantial money being allocated to vulnerable legislators, who may prove to be grateful or potentially malleable assets.

In Chapter 4, the importance of spending in Senate elections is discussed. Incumbents and challengers both benefit from spending in Senate elections. However, the rates of return from spending are not constant across incumbents, challengers, or parties. The effects of spending are curvilinear and indicate a decay in the dollar/vote benefit as spending increases. The ability of challengers and incumbents to raise and spend money is imperative to electoral success, and indicates that rent-seeking behavior to fund war chests is similarly rational. There is a point, however, where diminished returns from fund raising and spending are reached. The importance of candidate quality in determining election outcomes indicates that preemptive behavior by incumbents to either deter challengers or brace for tough contests is rational and leads incumbents to attempt to extract rents from monied interests.

Chapter 5 applies the lessons of the preceding analyses to the problem of campaign-finance reform. Proposed reforms of the campaign-finance system and congressional elections will not have the effect expected by their proponents. Reforms that fail to disrupt the rent-seeking ability of legislators and special interests will not succeed in effecting the desired change in the personnel of legislatures or in their behavior. Chapter 6 then discusses the prospects for eliminating rent seeking from a self-regulated monopoly.

1. The Senate in transition and campaign finance

> When, by the arbitrary power of the prince, the electors, or the ways of election, are altered, without the consent, and contrary to the common interest of the people, the *legislative is altered:* for, if others than those whom society hath authorized thereunto, do chuse, or in another way than what society hath prescribed, those chosen are not the legislative appointed by the people.
>
> John Locke
> *The Two Treatises of Government*

Adequate and fair representation has been at the center of the democratic debate in the United States since the Founding. In the intervening two centuries, a variety of disputes have arisen regarding the representative nature of the system, often attacking its real or perceived inequitable outcomes. Although the struggle for electoral participation by women and minorities has dominated the debate over representative democracy in the United States since the Civil War, how money affects elections and, therefore, the creation of public policy is also an important question. In this volume, we examine the role of money in campaigns for the contemporary U.S. Senate. Given the centrality of the Senate in policy making, combined with the tremendous powers enjoyed by individual Senators, it is appropriate to delineate the role played by money in contemporary Senate elections. In order to fully test the impact of rent seeking in the campaign-finance system on the political system, we also examine how rent-seeking behavior affects electoral outcomes. By modeling the role money plays in determining Senate election outcomes, we can assess the impact of recently proposed reforms of the campaign-finance system on Senatorial elections.

The U.S. Senate frequently has been characterized as a clubbish, collegial, inward-looking institution. Donald Matthews' classic *U.S.*

Senators and Their World (1960) noted that the strong "folkways" or norms of the Senate – such as seniority – performed a key function a generation ago in structuring its members' behavior. The allocation of virtually every resource ranging from committee positions to office space to debate privileges was determined by a member's seniority. The seniority norm was buttressed by other prominent norms, especially reciprocity, specialization, and freshman apprenticeship. These traditional legislative folkways fell especially heavily on new members. Junior Senators were expected to acquiesce to these norms and maintain a high degree of deference to senior members, especially committee chairs. As a result, prestige committees such as Armed Services, Appropriations, Finance, and Foreign Relations typically were dominated by senior members through the early 1960s.

Yet this image of the Senate seems alien to contemporary depictions. Barbara Sinclair's (1989) comprehensive study of the Senate since the 1970s finds that many of the norms of the U.S. Senate are substantially weakened or have disappeared entirely. In fact, this insular Senate vanished during the last quarter century. Junior members arrived in the Senate with established political agendas and regularly use floor privileges to pursue those agendas. Of the incumbent Senators in the 1980s, 25 percent possessed prior experience in the U.S. House of Representatives, and two-thirds of those members were elected to the House after 1974. Former governors account for 15 percent of incumbent Senators. Many other Senators with less prior governing experience have nonetheless used the Senate as an effective forum. Jeff Bingaman (D-NM) and Mitch McConnell (R-KY) pushed specific policy interests in a highly visible fashion after their arrival. Dan Quayle and Mark Andrews engaged in prominent issue fights with their party leadership and president during their initial terms of office (Fenno,1991a, 1989). More recently, Illinois Senator Carol Mosely Braun used the rules of debate to halt a pro forma renewal of the copyright for the logo of the Daughters of the Confederacy.

The massive increase in staff and other office resources also has liberated Senators from the more tedious research associated with legislative life (Malbin, 1980). As of 1989, the U.S. Senate had almost 6,000 full-time staffers. Only 20 percent of these staff were committee staff; the lion's share (3,837) were personal staff of legislators. Since 1979, the number of Senate staffers increased and then fell to the 1979 level. In that time, although there was no net change in the number of staffers, approximately 300 committee staff slots were eliminated and 245 new personal staff positions were added. The expansion of staff resources under the direct control of legislators, rather than committees, indicates a transfer of resources away from the creation of communal outputs from committees and toward discretionary use by individual entrepreneurs.

The shift in institutional behavior away from the traditional legislative norms of the previous era has been accompanied by a diffusion of power within the chamber. Reforms in committee assignment similarly have produced a Senate in which almost all members hold seats on prestige committees. Sinclair (1989), for example, notes that the relative number of seats on prestige committees held by junior legislators has increased substantially since 1974. Subcommittees increased substantially in number and legislative activity through 1976. The number of subcommittee assignments declined substantially from 1976 to 1978, and has since remained constant. Still, virtually every Senator now is either the ranking member or chair of a committee or subcommittee. Even as subcommittees declined in number after 1976, the average number of assignments per Senator actually increased (Ornstein, Mann, and Malbin, 1991). This has created multiple venues for exercising political power by all members. Senators are increasingly involved in legislative activity outside their formal areas of committee jurisdiction. Sinclair noted a substantial increase in floor amendment activity among noncommittee members since the 1960s. Increased staff resources have facilitated the ability of legislators to conduct investigations, research multiple policy arenas, and likewise deal with the large federal bureaucracy.

The decline of the apprenticeship and reciprocity norms have substantially increased floor activity and lengthened sessions. Incumbent Senators are more likely to employ filibuster threats, to increase amending activity, and to use holds[1] on pending legislation. For example, the ability of individual members such as Howard Metzenbaum to hold end-of-session legislation hostage with amending activities, quorum calls, and other legislative manipulations is legendary. The willingness to use such procedural powers underscores the ability of one Senator to frustrate the legislative process (See also Patterson and Kephart, 1992; Barone and Ujifusa, 1991).

Glenn Parker (1992b) argues that the evolution of the modern Congress is a result of the systematic expansion of discretion by lawmakers. As legislators expand into multiple issue areas, they are able to wield greater influence over multiple policy venues and exercise that influence on behalf of constituents, particular interests, or themselves. As greater numbers of legislators are able to actively participate in the legislative process, the attractiveness of the institution is enhanced. Therefore, legislators will attempt to create barriers to entry by challengers in order to protect their policy entrepreneur position and to preempt potentially strong challengers.

Interest groups and the Washington establishment

The transformation of the Senate in the last quarter century has been paralleled by the explosion of special-interest groups in Washington (Fiorina, 1989; Sinclair, 1989; Kingdon, 1984). The evolution of the nation's policy agenda from the 1950s to the 1970s spurred the emergence of expanded interest-group activity. The civil rights revolution, for instance, which attacked racial discrimination, opened the political agenda to a variety of other domestic social-welfare issues. Great Society legislation such as the Economic Opportunity Act of 1964, Medicare/Medicaid, and the Model Cities program expanded the federal government's role in employment practice, health care, and local government on an unprecedented scale (see also Sundquist, 1968). The environmental regulations of the 1970s produced legislation that similarly expanded the federal government's responsibilities in the areas of industrial and energy regulation (Regens, 1989). The dramatic alteration of the Washington policy community coincided with changes in the rewards system for Senators, thereby contributing to the evolution of senatorial behavior (Sinclair, 1989).

The expansion of the scope and magnitude of policy activity dramatically altered the incentives for interest groups to emerge and become active. The explosive growth of Washington-based interest groups between 1950 to 1980 is illustrated by the increase from 1,200 to over 7,000 in the number of groups in Washington (Sinclair, 1989; Salisbury, 1984). These myriad groups represent a diversity of interests on a variety of issues, and have produced a corresponding increase in lobbyists. For example, the success of consumer and environmental interest groups in spurring new regulations produced a counter-mobilization by the business community in the early 1970s. The number of corporations with Washington public-affairs offices quintupled to 500, and many firms expanded their existing Washington offices (Sinclair, 1989; Berry, 1984). Established business and corporate associations such as the National Association of Manufacturers increased their staff and lobbying efforts too. More recently, a similar countermobilization by the religious fundamentalist-driven New Right occurred in response to liberal social issues such as abortion, gay rights, and prayer in schools. Local and state governments established lobbying connections in Washington, at least partially in response to the increase in their mandated functions. Coinciding with the emergence of the special-interest group on the Washington policy scene, the past twenty years have seen a massive proliferation of political action committees (PACs).

The campaign-finance regime

The current campaign-finance regime is a product of legislation and of a series of court rulings of the 1970s. Contemporary campaign-finance regulations stem from the 1971 Federal Election Campaign Act (1971 FECA) and its 1974 amendments (1974 FECA). Prior to the passage of these laws, campaign contributions to congressional campaigns was regulated under a series of laws, primarily the Federal Corrupt Practices Act of 1925 (FCPA), and the Hatch Act amendments of 1940. Other provisions for campaign-finance regulation came from the Tillman Act of 1907 and the Labor Management Relations Act of 1947. The principle features of pre-1974 campaign-finance regulation included: the disclosure of receipts and expenditures by political committees operating in two or more states, and by House and Senate candidates; limits on contributions by individuals to federal candidates to $5000 per year to candidates or national committees connected to federal campaigns, and limited receipts to multistate political committees to $3,000,000 per year; limits on expenditures by House and Senate candidates and by political committees operating in more than two states; prohibiting monetary contributions from nationally chartered banks, corporations, and unions to any federal campaigns, and likewise prohibiting expenditures for activities in connection with such campaigns.

On the surface, these provisions appear to be fairly rigid. However, the system for financing election campaigns was often easily subverted, and its enforcement was haphazard. Cantor (1993, 1986), for instance, notes that from the enactment of the 1925 FCPA until its repeal in 1971 by the FECA, no candidate was ever prosecuted for violating federal campaign-finance laws. This offers strong circumstantial evidence that loopholes in the FCPA of 1925 were numerous and exploited with ease. Candidates would avoid contribution limits and disclosure rules by setting up numerous multistate committees, operating several committees within a single state, or establishing political committees in Washington, D.C., all of which were excluded from FCPA disclosure requirements (Cantor, 1986). Often, campaign contributors would channel funds through other family members to avoid the limits on disclosed contributions.[2] As a result, in his 1967 message to Congress, Lyndon Johnson referred to this campaign structure as being "more loophole than law " (Cantor and Huckabee, 1993).

The shortcomings in the 1925 law, combined with the subsequent Watergate scandal of 1972–4 prompted Congress to seek an alternative system to regulate the conduct of financing political campaigns at the federal level. The resulting changes in federal campaign finance led to the creation of the Federal Elections Commission (FEC), a bipartisan regulatory body whose members are appointed by the president subject to confirmation by the Senate. The FEC's primary function is to supervise and investigate violations of campaign-finance laws in congressional and presidential elections. The FEC has the ability to prosecute and levy civil penalties for violations of federal elections law, although that power has been used in only a limited way.

The 1971 and 1974 Federal Elections Campaign Acts

The initial attempt to reform federal campaign finance occurred in 1971. Provisions included in the Revenue Act of 1971 sought to lessen the dependence of presidential candidates on private money. The act established a federal subsidy of presidential campaigns starting with the 1976 election to be funded by a one-dollar federal income tax check off. A second bill, the Federal Elections Campaign Act of 1974, closed loop holes in the disclosure of contributions that were evident in the FCPA, and was intended to constrain "spiraling" campaign costs (Jacobson, 1975). The 1971 FECA established a quarterly reporting system, utilizing the secretaries of state of the various states and the clerk of the U.S. House and secretary of the U.S. Senate. Candidates were supposed to provide full disclosure for contributions of $100 or more and were required to provide notification within forty-eight hours of any contribution greater than $5,000. In addition, the legislation attempted to limit the amount of money candidates could expend on media advertising ($50,000) and required broadcasters to sell commercial time during the election period at lowest-unit-rate (LUR) prices.

The Watergate scandal of 1972–4 demonstrated the shortcomings of the 1971 legislation and served as a catalyst for even more extensive campaign-finance reform under the 1974 FECA amendments. Given the aura of conspiracy surrounding the Watergate break-in and its ensuing cover-up, congressional and media investigators as well as the public were regaled with stories of large cash donations to the Committee to Re-Elect the President and of bagmen dropping money into the hands of influentials in the Nixon campaign (White, 1976). Congressional supporters of more sweeping changes in the campaign-finance system were able to capitalize on the widespread outrage generated by the Watergate scandal as a lever to pass strong campaign-finance reform (White, 1976). The result of these efforts, the 1974 FECA amendments, is the basis for the existing campaign-finance regulatory system.

The 1974 FECA amendments limited contributions by individual donors to $1,000 per candidate per election. They also established regulations governing the formation and activities of PACs. Political action committees and party committees were prohibited from contributing more than $5,000 per candidate per election. In addition, the FECA amendments instituted spending limits for all federal elections, indexed to inflation, of $70,000 in House elections and of $150,000 or $0.12 per voter, whichever is greater, in Senate elections. These limits on overall congressional spending, however, were overturned in *Buckley v. Valeo* [424 U.S. 1 (1976)] as a violation of freedom of expression protected under the First Amendment, although limits on contributions by individuals are permissible.

The 1976 FECA amendments reconstituted the FEC, and established additional guidelines for individuals, party committees, and PAC activity. Under the 1976 amendments, the limit on individual donations to PACs was increased to $5,000, whereas the cap on donations to party committees was increased to $20,000. A loop hole in PAC regulation was closed by limiting contributions from all PACs sponsored by the same organization to $5,000 per candidate. This effectively treats related committees as one entity. Rules governing the solicitation of funds by labor, corporate, and trade association PACs were more clearly delineated.

The primary purpose of the campaign-finance reforms of the 1970s was to increase accountability and visibility of money given to candidates for political office. Presumably, by placing strict limits on individual and organization contributions and by requiring disclosure of any substantial donations, the significant amounts of money provided by individuals into federal elections might be reduced. Despite such promises offered by its sponsors, the creation of the PAC system has not produced a small-money, low-cost system of elections. Instead, campaign costs have continued to spiral upward. As a result, congressional candidates are devoting even more time to raising money to seek or retain office.

Origins of political action committees

The legality of forming PACs was established by the Supreme Court's ruling in *Pipefitters Local #52 v. the United States*. Before the *Pipefitters Local* case, contributions by labor organizations to federal candidates were banned under the Taft-Hartley Act of 1947.

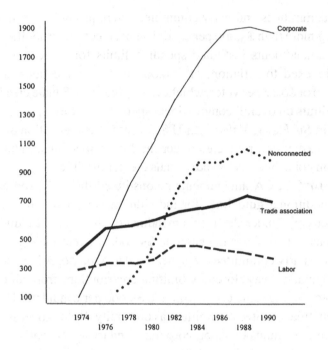

Figure 1.1 *Trends in PAC growth, 1974–90*

Corporations similarly were prohibited from making direct campaign contributions under the Tillman Act of 1907. Although labor unions quickly moved to form a number of PACs (most notably the legendary Congress of Industrial Operators [CIO–PAC]), corporations were less prone to do so, primarily because there were no clear regulations governing the conditions under which corporate PACs might operate. The passage of the 1974 and 1976 Federal Election Campaign Act amendments clarified the grounds under which corporations and trade associations could form PACs. As Figure 1.1 shows, this was followed by a dramatic increase in PACs (Stanley and Niemi, 1992; Sabato, 1985), especially corporate PACs (Wilhite and Paul, 1989). Most of the growth in PACs has been among corporations (1,706 additional PACs since 1974) and trade associations (456 more PACs since 1974) and non-connected-issue PACs (952 more PACs from 1978 to 1991).

Table 1.1. *The increasing costs of Senate campaigns, 1980-1992*

Year	Total expenditures		PAC receipts		Party support[a]	
	Total	Mean	Total	Mean	Total	Mean
1980						
Democrats	67,229,236	1,977,331	7,343,262	215,978	1,613,376	39,540
Republicans	56,334,117	1,707,095	8,383,970	254,060	6,096,762	184,750
1982						
Democrats	86,469,805	2,620,285	10,839,451	328,468	2,844,534	86,198
Republicans	76,861,816	2,329,146	10,951,593	331,866	9,315,982	282,302
1984						
Democrats	84,887,721	2,572,355	12,975,151	393,186	4,389,198	133,006
Republicans	95,981,320	2,999,416	14,914,866	466,490	7,108,137	222,151
1986						
Democrats	93,260,574	2,742,958	19,854,841	583,966	7,276,118	214,003
Republicans	95,981,320	3,998,596	24,722,545	727,134	10,807,424	317,865
1988						
Democrats	113,152,383	3,428,860	23,194,684	702,869	6,998,371	212,072
Republicans	102,690,751	3,111,841	21,203,072	642,517	10,953,102	331,912
1990						
Democrats	89,485,296	2,711,676	19,886,031	602,607	5,722,089	173,397
Republicans	94,958,012	2,877,515	20,923,878	634,057	8,533,001	258,576
1992						
Democrats	98,631,025	2,818,029	24,377,538	696,501	11,461,165	327,462
Republicans	96,698,298	2,844,068	20,738,868	609,967	16,171,332	475,627

[a.] Coordinated expenditures and direct contributions from party committees.

Source: Federal Elections Commission. All financial data are expressed in constant 1992 dollars.

Doubt remains whether the net impact of the 1974 reforms on the U.S. political system has been positive. As the political system has been "opened" to more individual and special-interest participation, campaign costs have spiraled upward, far outstripping the rate of inflation. As Table 1.1 illustrates, despite a temporary decline from 1988 to 1990, the overall expenditures by candidates increased substantially after 1980. The dramatic increase in PAC contributions is particularly noteworthy. The rate of increase in PAC contributions to candidates has outstripped the rate of increase in spending elections. In fact, controlling for inflation, expenditures in Senate elections have increased by 58 percent, whereas PAC contributions to Senate candidates have increased by approximately 200 percent. Contrary to conventional wisdom, the increase in PAC support is especially evident among Democratic candidates, whose contributions from PACs increased by 214 percent from 1980 to 1992. At the same time, incumbents enjoyed high levels of electoral security, although this phenomenon was initially more evident in House than in Senate races (Abramowitz, 1980).

Reflecting this trend, PACs have become a common target of critics of Congress and the campaign-finance system. The proliferation of these committees is viewed as the primary source for the increase in money flowing into congressional campaigns, although most Senate candidates raise more money from individuals than from PACs (see also Jacobson, 1989). When the selective interests PACs represent, coupled with the large amounts of money they give to candidates in the aggregate, are considered, the perception of a corrupting or illicit influence by special interests over legislators emerges (Etzioni, 1990). However, the growth of PACs and the increase in money provided to Senate candidates may only be reflections of campaigning in contemporary society (Campbell, Alford, and Henry, 1984).[3]

The increased use of television, targeted mail, and other technologies that allow those candidates to reach voters are expensive (Godwin, 1992; Ansolabehere, Behr, and Iyengar, 1992). Office resources such as mailings or trips home are not necessarily sufficient to maintain the image of an invulnerable incumbent; therefore, campaign messages are commonly communicated in the electronic media via purchased airtime. Although political candidates are permitted to purchase advertising at the bottom-of-rate-card prices, the sheer volume of advertising in Senate elections is dictated by the financial resources available to the candidate. In essence, to buy airtime, the politician must pursue fund-raising opportunities. Although the existing campaign-finance regime offers equal opportunity of candidates to raise money from a variety of sources, this system does not offer equality of ability in fund raising, nor does it prevent candidates from leveraging personal or official assets to obtain financial support.[4]

One useful way of visualizing this system is to view legislators as firms in a competitive market. Legislators are elected from individual constituencies. In the process of election, a series of market transactions take place that influence the shape of government via choosing a representative. Voters cast ballots for individuals and are presumed to be expressing a set of policy preferences by supporting a particular candidate (Downs, 1957; Arrow, 1951). These preferences may be shaped by a variety of factors including the ideal candidate or policy package, as well as perceptions of the candidate most proximate to that ideal (see Enelow and Hinich, 1984).

The legislator, by winning election, has obtained a proprietary position in the policy process. In effect, the candidates assume positions in a cartel from which policy can be provided. They are members of a policy oligopoly that provides benefits to particular interests that transcend physical constituencies.5 The provision of policy is not limited to the geographical constituencies represented by a legislator, nor is the provision of benefits limited to those interests that are physically located in the legislator's constituency. Therefore, interest groups have incentives to develop access and influence with a variety of legislators (Kingdon, 1984). This may make it possible for incumbent legislators to capture campaign contributions whose dollar value exceeds the level of funding necessary to contest successfully their next election: They will potentially be able to garner rents.

Rent-seeking interests and the legislator

Acting through PACs, rent-seeking interests will follow one of two strategies to access lawmakers and influence the provision of policy to obtain government outputs as particularized benefits (Wright, 1989; Denzau and Munger, 1986):

1. Interests may attempt to change the composition of government in order to obtain benefits. Pursuit of this course of action necessitates two of three preexisting conditions. First, the particular interest must be unable to obtain the desired benefit or regulation from the incumbent legislature. Second, the costs of changing the legislature and then obtaining desired benefits are less than the costs of influencing the existing government to produce benefits. Third, the opposition must appear capable of providing a reasonable performance in the election and be willing to provide the desired benefits.

2. Interests may attempt to influence the incumbent government to produce the selective benefit. In order for this to occur, the government must be receptive to the influence of a particularized interest, and the costs of the transaction for the interest group must not be too high compared to the benefit. Individual legislators

Table 1.2. *Distribution of incumbents seeking reelection by party, 1978-92*

Year	Democrats		Republicans		Percentage running
	Running	Not running	Running	Not running	
1978	9	7	11	6	60.6
1980	18	6	9	1	79.4
1982	18	1	11	3	87.9
1984	12	2	17	2	87.9
1986	9	3	19	3	82.4
1988	17	3	11	3	84.8
1990	16	0	14	3	94.1
1992	17	3	12	2	85.3

Source: Congressional Quarterly Weekly Report: Election Preview Issues (1978-92 inclusive).

and specific interests must be willing to bend from ideologically motivated behavior and instead pursue "pragmatic" strategies.

If the former strategy is pursued, interests will attempt to support and elect candidates who are receptive to their political or regulatory preferences. If so, candidates will receive support regardless of their incumbency status, and monied interests could even shop for potential candidates to challenge incumbents. Instead, expressed candidate preferences will be the criteria by which allocations occur. If the latter strategy is pursued, interests may bend ideological or "pure" motivations in order to extract benefits from the existing government, especially if the costs of physically changing the incumbents in government are too high.

Recalling our assumption that rents increase as the supply curve becomes more vertical (Figure 1.1 – in the Introduction), it is clear that the Constitution establishes a fixed supply of Senate seats available to contest in a given election cycle. Although the supply of prospective challengers may be infinitely elastic under perfect competition, general elections commonly involve a two-candidate setting in U.S.

politics with the incumbent typically opting to seek reelection. Since 1978, over 80 percent of the eligible incumbents sought to retain their seats whereas less than 20 percent voluntarily retired (see Table 1.2). Viewed in this light, the vertical line A in Figure I.1 effectively represents the supply of either available Senate seats or incumbent Senators seeking reelection in a given cycle. The relative success achieved by those incumbents as well as trends in campaign contributions to winning challengers reveals that few low-cost substitutes exist (Abramowitz and Segal, 1992). Because of the relatively fixed supply and the imperfect competition created by incumbency advantages, this implies that incumbents may be well positioned to seek rents in the form of campaign contributions.

The precise determination of which legislators obtained rents requires some elaboration. Because virtually all legislators received some form of financial contribution from the relevant PACs, the definition of any receipt as a rent renders all Senators successful rent seekers. However, it is also clear that Senators differ in the amount of campaign contributions received from various PACs and individuals (Regens, Gaddie, and Elliott, 1994, 1993; Sabato, 1985). Variation in receipts among members of the Senate provides a better criterion for identifying the precise nature of rents acquired. Viewing legislators as potential rent-seeking agents allows us to better understand how Senators provide selective individual benefits that add to the dead-weight loss of society and create or propagate policies that may run counter to the desires of their geographical constituencies or the collective good (see Denzau and Munger, 1986).

A variety of goods and services are provided to legislators that might be construed as rents. Some of these are no longer permissible for legislators, although the availability of these benefits in the past indicates that their receipt might be construed as captured rents. In the broadest of terms, a rent can be defined as any profit gained beyond the marginal cost of producing a good or service. That is, rents are "extra income," including the payment of honoraria income and campaign contributions (Regens, Gaddie, and Elliott, 1994, 1993; Parker, 1992a, 1992b; Regens, Elliott, and Gaddie, 1991; Grier and Munger, 1991; Grier, Munger, and Torrent, 1990; Munger, 1989). Viewed in this light, a variety of financial and pseudofinancial transfers have occurred that pay legislators "rents" for policy outputs. Fritz and Morris (1992) have extensively documented the use of campaign expenditures by legislators for a variety of noncampaign-related personal benefits, which the legislators exploit. Fact-finding junkets and sponsored donations might also be construed as rents, because the legislator derives positive benefits (albeit not cash benefits) from these activities that arise from their position in the policy cartel. One of the most blatant examples of rent acquisition is the now defunct loophole in campaign-finance law regarding the disposition of the war chests of retiring incumbents. Until 1993, legislators elected prior to 1981 were able to retire while retaining their often sizeable war chests for personal or charitable use. Given the record number of House retirements in 1992, many legislators appear to have opted out of the Congress in order to "cash in their chips."

Another rent available to successful politicians is the political office itself. It is plausible that the benefits captured simply by virtue of holding office constitute rents (Paul and Wilhite, 1990; Wilhite and Paul, 1989) . Because politicians seek to externalize the costs of their venture by raising contributions and enjoy added benefits from the office, attaining political office is a successful rent-seeking venture, although legislators are able to accrue those benefits only as long as they hold office.[6] Senators who are able to remain in office and are likely to continue to do so in the future constitute the "best bet" for investors. Given the importance of money to electoral outcomes (Jacobson, 1992, 1990, 1985; Squire, 1991, 1989; Krasno and Green, 1988; Green and Krasno, 1988), incumbents who attempt to retain their Senate seats have a vested interest in seeking excessive financial support to deter viable challengers and sustain an image of invulnerability (Squire, 1991). To do otherwise increases the probability of losing office and therefore heightens the likelihood of losing influence in the policy market. The office can also serve as a vehicle for higher office. Because political office holding at a lower level enhances the ability to move successfully to the next level, the greater public profile enjoyed by holding public office is part of the captured rent.

In the remainder of this volume we model the behavior of U.S. Senators as rent-seeking agents in a self-regulating market.[7] Changing patterns in the allocation of campaign contributions are examined to support our theory of legislators as competitors in a policy market. We also explore the shifting behavior of legislators regarding the timing of fund raising within election cycles and amount of campaign contributions raised which reinforce the picture of legislators as competing in the policy market to retain their elective office. The results of these analyses lend greater understanding of the policy process and the behavior of legislators. The findings of these chapters should indicate the limits of reform in a rent-seeking society.

2. Early money and profit taking in Senate campaigns

As one-third would go out triennially, there would always be divisions holding their places for unequal terms and consequently acting under the influence of different views and different impulses.

James Madison
Notes of Debates in the Federal Convention of 1787

Among those "different views and different impulses" is the impulse to campaign for reelection. In a cyclical view of the matter, the impulse would be strongest in the class for which election day was closest at hand.

Richard F. Fenno
The United States Senate: A Bicameral Perspective

Political scientists have devoted substantial energy to describing the roles played by the major political parties as well as political action committees (PACs) in funding congressional campaigns. Mirroring the assumption succinctly expressed by Madison in *The Federalist Number 10* that self-interest motivates political behavior, the national parties and PACs have a strong incentive to provide financial support to their preferred candidates (Herrnson, 1989; Eismeier and Pollack, 1986a, 1986b). Under existing campaign regulations, we can readily observe similar benefit-seeking behavior among politicians, especially incumbents who attempt to exploit their office to garner financial support (Jacobson, 1989; Sabato, 1985). Although a myriad of factors may influence the ability of incumbents to acquire campaign contributions (see Munger, 1989; Poole and Romer, 1985; Gopoian, 1984), the conventional wisdom and empirical research suggest the motivation for legislators to engage in those market exchanges is primarily to protect their reelection prospects (Fiorina, 1989; Mayhew, 1974). Because successful candidates can retain their cash on hand at the end of an election cycle for use in a subsequent one, those assets are a tangible, personal benefit paid to incumbents in the U.S. Congress.

Interestingly enough, however, the fact that those campaign funds represent a potential source of "extra" compensation, or rents, has received scant scholarly attention (see Parker, 1992a). We contend that the campaign-finance process functions as a quasimarket for the provision and extraction of additional compensation by legislators and particular interests (Regens, Gaddie, and Elliott, 1994; Grier and Munger, 1991; Denzau and Munger, 1986; Becker, 1983). Our underlying assumption is that legislators, acting in their role as policy makers, are able to obtain campaign contributions in excess of their opportunity costs to acquire such support because they are able to distribute collective or public goods as selective benefits that contributors compete to receive (Denzau and Munger, 1986; Posner, 1974; Stigler, 1971). For example, recent research on the influence of interest-groups notes that monetary exchanges in the form of PAC contributions buy access and reward "friends," and therefore create an opportunity to influence the policy-making process (Regens, Gaddie and Elliott, 1994, 1993; Regens, Elliott and Gaddie, 1991; Wright, 1989). Moreover, like any profit-seeking firm, legislators have vested interest in maintaining their market position vis-à-vis the provision of, or influence over, government outputs.[1] Because all legislators are not equally successful in shaping policy choices or maintaining their elective office, we expect the ability to acquire campaign funds to vary among members. For this reason, we assume that the allocation of campaign contributions to legislators, and the efforts by those legislators to acquire financial rewards, respond to supply and demand considerations.[2]

Of course, just as rent seeking by firms in the market can be inefficient (see Tollison, 1982; Buchanan, 1980; Tullock, 1980b), it is plausible for the efforts and expenditures of potential recipients of political contributions to produce waste in the process of pursuing both campaign support and the policy oligopoly position that a successful campaign offers as reward. Legislators at all levels often raise far more money than necessary for reelection. However, many often expend substantial efforts seeking campaign support and still are confronted by debt at the end of an election. For incumbents who run races at a cost less than the size of their war chest, the remaining surplus constitutes an acquired asset which can be converted to quasi-legal, noncampaign benefits; or these monies can be squirreled away for a future campaign. To test for such waste, in this section we examine the extent to which incumbent U.S. Senators are able to retain their seat and likewise create a "profit" from their campaign (i.e., are efficient rent seekers).

Under perfect competitive conditions without friction or information constraints, a candidate could forecast the financial support necessary to seek reelection, and spend sufficient effort to raise money at a level to ensure reelection. In this world, because incumbents campaign under conditions of less than perfect information, fund raising is inexact and overruns in expenditures or receipts are possible. We examine the 1984–90 election cycles in order to test empirically the actual efficiency of Senate incumbents in profit taking in the form of campaign contributions.

The enhanced visibility of a Senate seat and the lengthy term of office between elections may lead prospective contributors to view Senators as more stable assets for seeking entree into the policy arena, thereby increasing both the value of a Senator's output and the magnitude of campaign contributions (Parker, 1992a). Incumbents also possess nonelectoral priorities that may drive profit taking under the guise of campaign fund raising. Moreover, to the extent incumbents are generally successful against their electoral challengers (see Fiorina, 1989), they typically are the best investment option for groups seeking entree to policy making. This may allow incumbents to demand and then extract substantial campaign support. These institutional and behavioral factors further enhance the image of the Senate as an institution whose members are potentially well-positioned to extract sizable personal benefits solely on the basis of their incumbency.

The Senate offers an interesting laboratory for examining the dynamics of campaign finance in U.S. elections. Senators traditionally have enjoyed lulls in campaigning and fund raising, whereas House members historically have been plagued by year-round fund raising and continuous campaigning due to the short term of office (see Jacobson, 1990; Fiorina, 1989). However, just when scholarship focused on the Senate, the behavior of Senators evolved. Changes in senatorial behavior are especially evident in the area of campaign fund raising. Fenno (1982) noted that Senate incumbents prior to the

1980s were prone to engage in limited fund raising during the first two years of their term. Fund raising then dropped off during the midterm before increasing substantially during the final two years of the term. Over the past twenty years, Senators accelerated early fund raising, coinciding with the dramatic increase in costs of U.S. Senate campaigns (Sorauf, 1988). Senators seem to have responded to the increasing costs associated with campaigning for reelection by engaging in substantial fund raising well in advance of election day. Why would Senators increase fund raising three or even five years before reelection? Senators have only some notion of who their next opponent will be and may not even be certain they will seek reelection. House members who moved to the Senate often note that the longer election cycle allows them to focus more on policy, rather than spending most of their time engaged in constant electioneering (Fenno, 1989). Despite this shift in fund-raising activity, recent research suggests that no preemptive electoral benefit is derived from early fund raising (Squire, 1991); nonetheless, incumbents pursue early money. Even with controls for inflation, Senators substantially increased their early money receipts during the 1980s.

In this chapter, we model cyclical fund raising by Senate incumbents running for reelection in the 1983–4 through 1989–90 election cycles. By examining cyclical fund-raising trends, we will be better able to understand who engages in early fund raising and why they do so. We uncover partisan and temporal trends in early fund raising from individual and PAC sources. Those characteristics of incumbents that are indicative of early fund raising from PAC and individual sources are identified. We then test the assumptions made under the rent-seeking paradigm in a multivariate model. Then, given the lack of a meaningful impact by preemptive fund raising on challenger profiles (Squire, 1991), we offer a model of efficient profit taking that has its origins in early fund raising. The rent-acquisition model of early fund raising is then tested and discussed.

Why raise early money?

For most of the twentieth century, the conventional wisdom held that the U.S. Senate was the more "serious" legislative body, at least partially due to the impact of the longer legislative terms served by Senators. Senators, unlike their counterparts in the House, were thought to be better protected from the rapid tides of political change. In fact, this viewpoint has deep roots in the nation's political history. George Washington, during a conversation with Thomas Jefferson in Paris, explained the bicameral notion with Jefferson's own act of pouring coffee into a saucer. "Why," asked Washington, "did you pour your coffee into your saucer?" "To cool it," replied Jefferson. "Even so," said Washington, "pour legislation into the Senatorial saucer to cool it" (Fenno, 1982). In effect, a Senator was expected to devote attention to lawmaking while remaining isolated from campaigning and constituency politics throughout most of the term. This pattern of campaign activity is reflected in the pattern of fund raising illustrated in Figure 2.1, which depicts fund raising as a curvilinear function with a midterm trough (Fenno, 1982).

More recently, Squire (1991) noted the dramatic increase in off-year cash raised by incumbent Senators and identified some of the indicators of preemptive fund raising during the early 1980s. In particular, Squire found that Senators who were from larger states or who faced larger pools of potential quality challengers were more likely to engage in preemptive fund raising during off-cycle years.[3] Yet, even with challengers making increasingly early decisions to enter races (Patterson and Kephart, 1992), Fenno's assumption that preemptive fund raising is designed to deter strong potential challengers is not borne out in Squire's analysis. Instead, Squire found no impact by preemptive fund raising on the profile of challengers to incumbent Senators. Why, then, are Senators raising so much early money?

An alternative rationale is available in the literature on interest-group influence. Denzau and Munger (1986) hypothesize that legislators have a "price" for which they will provide policy outputs to particularized interests and that this price is dependent on the marginal cost to provide the policy. Presumably, legislators who can influence policy outputs at relatively low costs are positioned to extract substantial financial compensation such as campaign contributions or honoraria (see Parker, 1992a; Fritz and Morris, 1992). In fact, empirical research demonstrates that there is substantial variation among Senators in terms of their ability to leverage their policy po-

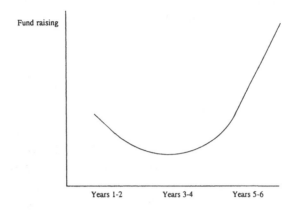

Figure 2.1. *Fenno's cyclical pattern of fund raising by Senators*

sitions into financial remuneration (Parker, 1992a; Grier and Munger, 1991; Grier, Munger, and Torrent, 1990). Several studies indicate corporate and trade-association interests with economic incentives to influence policy appear to be quite adept at identifying and rewarding legislators who can create particularized benefits through policy (Regens, Gaddie, and Elliott, 1994, 1993; Munger, 1989; Gopoian, 1984); and large sums of campaign money are spent by incumbents on nonelectoral activities. This suggests that Senators have motives to raise substantial campaign funds that go beyond their electoral needs (Fritz and Morris, 1992; Parker, 1992a).

For Senators, nonelection-year cycles offer opportunities to provide benefits selectively to particular interests at relatively low costs. Senators who are not seeking reelection are, nonetheless, still able to provide policy outputs. The political costs to an incumbent in terms of constituency support for providing a policy benefit may be lower in nonelection-cycle years. This is plausible since Senators have extremely visible profiles in their constituencies, which make their activities subject to almost universal scrutiny (Fenno, 1982; Abramowitz, 1980). As a result, the likelihood that providing a particularized benefit will fade from the public memory decreases as the temporal proximity of reelection increases. Thus, the marginal cost of providing selective benefits will be lower in nonelection cycles because the potential reelection sanction for the legislator of providing policy is likely to decay over time, if costs are born at all.

Evidence of early fund raising

Previous research has focused on the aggregate level of early funding obtained by U.S. Senators prior to the election-year cycle. In order to better understand the intricacies of early fund raising, we disaggregate early money allocations by source and cycle. Analyses are conducted on funds raised from all sources in the early cycles (years 1 and 2), middle cycles (years 3 and 4), and reelection cycles (years 5 and 6) of Senate terms. Then, separate analyses are conducted on funds raised from PACs and from individuals in each cycle. The results of this analysis should illuminate the incentive system that drives incumbent fund raising, because the intuitive electoral benefits of such activity are not empirically evident (Squire, 1991).

Although early fund raising initially was pursued by Democratic incumbents in the 1970s, Republicans became increasingly adept at early fund raising in the 1980s. Since 1979–80, Republican Senators raise more money on average in early cycles than do their Democratic counterparts. Republicans also raise more money in the middle cycles of their terms for every cycle except 1981–2 (see Table 2.1). In essence, the shift toward perpetual fund raising obliterated Fenno's trough among Democrats in 1979–80, and for Republican incumbents running for reelection in 1986, 1988, and 1990.

Closer examination of the campaign contribution patterns of Senators reveals that in 38 instances Senators raised less money in the middle cycle of their term than in the early cycle, whereas 63 increased fund raising in the middle cycle from the first cycle. Of the 38 Senators who decreased fund raising after the early cycle, 14 (all of whom were successful) were seeking reelection in 1990. Democrats more frequently increased fund raising from early to middle cycles in the early 1980s, although 7 of the 14 incumbents who decreased fund raising from the early cycle to the middle cycle in their term were Democrats. Overall, only 15 of the 38 Senators whose fund-raising pattern demonstrated Fenno's midterm trough were Democrats.

Table 2.1. *Average receipts by U.S. Senators, by party and source, 1979-90*

	Cycle in term of office		
	Early	Middle	Reelection
Cohort/party	(Years 1-2)	(Years 3-4)	(Years 5-6)
Total receipts			
1979-84 Republicans	232.5	178.3	3,890.0
1979-84 Democrats	78.8	270.9	2,331.9
1981-86 Republicans	234.5	594.4	4,240.4
1981-86 Democrats	146.8	222.0	3,484.5
1983-88 Republicans	356.9	613.5	4,401.9
1983-88 Democrats	237.0	480.5	3,914.0
1985-90 Republicans	458.2	588.5	3,652.4
1985-90 Democrats	351.6	453.9	3,862.9
Individual receipts			
1979-84 Republicans	137.6	124.5	2,796.2
1979-84 Democrats	43.7	163.1	1,452.6
1981-86 Republicans	113.4	439.0	2,887.8
1981-86 Democrats	64.1	125.9	2,318.5
1983-88 Republicans	238.1	429.6	2,947.9
1983-88 Democrats	88.6	307.2	2,541.6
1985-90 Republicans	206.1	475.9	2,567.3
1985-90 Democrats	243.6	314.6	2,642.7
PAC receipts			
1979-84 Republicans	50.6	30.8	847.9
1979-84 Democrats	17.7	47.4	677.4
1981-86 Republicans	48.9	104.4	1,085.0
1981-86 Democrats	36.0	67.7	902.1
1983-88 Republicans	72.7	131.3	1,258.2
1983-88 Democrats	63.2	132.6	1,151.5
1985-90 Republicans	40.1	56.9	828.2
1985-90 Democrats	38.0	78.6	992.4

All financial data are expressed in thousands of constant 1990 dollars.
Source: Federal Elections Commission.

Incumbent Senators typically engaged in virtually continuous fund raising from individual donors throughout the period under study. Although Republicans had a slight lull in the average funds raised from individuals in the 1979–84 class, this was reversed with the next class of Republican Senators, who substantially increased their average receipts from individuals from the early cycle to middle cycle in every class of Senators after the 1979–84 class. Among Democrats, fund raising from individuals always increased from the beginning of the term to the middle of the term, but the size of these increases is not as great as among Republicans.

Political action committees were not immune to increased early fund raising by Senate incumbents. Republican incumbents generally raised more PAC money than Democrats in every early cycle from 1979–80 to 1985–6. Republicans raised less money from PACs in the middle cycle of the 1979–84 cohort and the 1985–90 cohort, and raised approximately the same amount of money per incumbent as Democrats in the middle cycle of the 1983–8 class. Although the average amount of early money raised by both Republicans and Democrats was much higher from individuals than from PACs, approximately a third of the Senators seeking reelection obtained more contributions from PACs than from individuals in the early cycle of their term. A similar number of incumbents obtained more PAC money than individual contributions during middle cycles.

Senators whose PAC receipts exceeded individual contributions in the early cycle of a term were usually Republicans (23 of 37 cases), wheras incumbents who generally raised more PAC money than individual money in middle cycles were Democrats (20 of 34 cases). One possible explanation for the decline in early- and middle-cycle fund raising in 1981–2 is that traditionally Republican donors were funding Republican House incumbents, many of whom were vulnerable to the effects of the economic recession (Jacobson and Kernell, 1983). It is plausible that the decreased Republican funding in all cycles after 1986 – especially from PACs – can be attributed in part to the GOP loss of control of the U.S. Senate (see Regens, Gaddie, and Elliott, 1994).

Multivariate analysis

The previous section described a substantial shift in the fund-raising patterns of incumbent Senators in non-reelection-cycle years (see also Squire, 1991). The lull between early-cycle and reelection-cycle fund raising observed by Fenno has disappeared. From the moment a Senator is reelected, a process of sustained fund raising begins that only becomes more intense and produces ever increasing revenue as the next election draws nearer (see Figure 2.2). The descriptive analysis noted partisan and source differences in non-reelection-cycle fund raising by U.S. Senators. The analysis does not indicate why certain

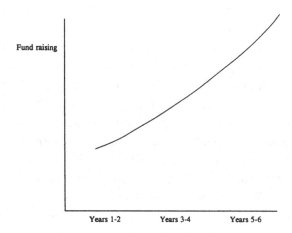

Figure 2.2. *Observed fund-raising behavior by Senators since 1978*

incumbents raise more early money among individuals instead of PACs or which members have increased middle-cycle fund raising. A variety of electoral, personal, and constituency attributes may contribute to the pursuit of early fund raising by incumbents and may influence the choice of source from which incumbents attempt to obtain money.

Electoral insecurity is an obvious rationale for incumbents to raise substantial money early in a term. PACs and individuals contribute more to electorally vulnerable Senators due to increased efforts by those Senators to attract funds. According to our theory, PACs should view vulnerable Senators as highly productive, albeit potentially short-term, investments (Denzau and Munger, 1986). Alternatively, those Senate incumbents whose prior margin of victory suggests they are relatively "safe" from strong challenges may seek to extract early support based on the relatively low constituency costs they perceive in providing such benefits (Parker, 1992a).

Attributes of Senate challengers also may impact on an incumbent's ability to capture campaign contributions from individual donors or PACs. Squire (1991, 1989) found highly experienced challengers more likely to emerge in states where the opposite party holds large numbers of congressional seats and statewide offices. The size of challenger pools was related to the increase in aggregate early fund raising by Senate incumbents. This suggests that Senators facing large challenger pools were more likely to engage in ever-increasing fund raising among PACs and individuals. These incumbents may be even more likely to pursue PAC money, due to the larger amounts of money that PACs can direct into candidate campaigns and the increased likelihood that they will face a strong challenger. By comparison, Senators who invest effort in the early acquisition of support from individuals may be building up "rainy day" money for an unseen, potentially strong challenger. Because these members are not driven by immediate electoral needs or vulnerability, they do not have to sell policy to organized interests.

As we noted in the descriptive analysis, party affiliation may be related to the propensity of Senators to raise early money. Republican incumbents are generally more adept at raising money throughout electoral cycles, although this talent is more pronounced in extracting funds from individuals than from PACs.

Early-cycle fund raising may be related to the financial position of incumbent Senators at the end of their last reelection attempt. Fenno (1982) noted that incumbents engaged in more fund raising in early cycles than in middle cycles because they sought to replenish depleted war chests or to retire debt. Therefore, the financial position of an incumbent at the beginning of an electoral cycle may motivate heavy fund raising to replenish a war chest or retire debt. We include measures of both the incumbent cash on hand and debt at the beginning of each two-year election cycle to capture these effects.[4]

Although there has been a long-term decentralization of power and authority, the leadership continues to play a major agenda-setting role in the contemporary Senate. Accordingly, being in a leadership position should be associated with receiving substantial support in terms of campaign contributions.

Reflecting advancement patterns in terms of the relative prestige of electoral offices, a number of incumbent Senators (25.2%) have prior service as House members. Among those Senate incumbents seeking reelection during the series of cycles from 1984 to 1990, 15.6 percent moved directly from the House to the Senate in 1978 or later. Those individuals may have carried with them the almost continual electioneering and fund-raising habits typical of the lower chamber.

As a result, former Representatives may be more adept at fund raising than their counterparts lacking House service.

Although many norms of behavior have lapsed during the last two decades, freshman legislators often follow a variety of cues from their peers. Massive preemptive fund raising may be evident among all Senators who have just entered the chamber. However, these members may be more adept at fund raising from PACs rather than individuals, if only because freshmen may be considered more malleable assets by particularized interests. Therefore, we include a variable indicating freshman Senators seeking reelection (see also Grier and Munger, 1991).

As Squire (1989) has shown, state size is related to the level of expenditures made by Senate candidates for their election campaigns, and Nagler and Leighley (1992) have documented the importance of population in TV campaign expenditures. Studies by Jacobson (1975) and Campbell, Alford, and Henry (1984) indicate that media market dissemination and congruence with the population are important factors in congressional elections. Given the relationship between media, population, and money, it seems reasonable to assume that incumbents are likely to pursue campaign contributions to insulate themselves against the costs of maintaining their seats in a large state.

In addition to these theoretically plausible variables, we include a temporal counter. This permits us to control for long-term growth in fund raising that may be related to the general increase in campaign costs (Campbell and Sumners, 1990; Abramowitz, 1989).

Because the dependent variable is continuous, we estimated the following equation using ordinary least squares (OLS) to test our assumptions:

$$Y = a + b_1X_1 + b_2X_2 + b_3X_3 + b_4X_4 + b_5X_5 + b_6X_6 + b_7X_7 + b_8X_8 + b_9X_9 + b_{10}X_{10} + e \qquad [1]$$

where

X_1 = incumbent cash on hand at the beginning of the cycle analyzed, expressed in constant 1990 dollars

X_2 = incumbent debt at the beginning of the analyzed cycle, expressed in constant 1990 dollars

X_3 = dummy variable for party coded 1 if Republican, and 0 otherwise

X_4 = dichotomous variable coded 1 for any member who previously served in the House of Representatives

X_5 = margin of previous reelection victory, defined as 50 percent minus the candidate's total percentage of the two-party vote

X_6 = polytomous dummy variable coded 1 for any member in committee leadership positions (committee chair, ranking member), 2 for members of the floor leadership, and 0 otherwise (see also Parker, 1992a)

X_7 = dichotomous variable coded 1 if the member is a freshman, and 0 otherwise

X_8 = challenger pool, measured as the total number of congressmen and statewide elected officials who are members of the opposite party

X_9 = state-media market size and dispersion index, calculated by multiplying the number of TV households in a state (in thousands) by the dispersal of TV households among local markets

X_{10} = a continuous counter ranging from 1 to 4, representing each election cycle from 1984 to 1990.

The results of the OLS analyses are presented in three parts. First, we discuss those factors that account for variation in the total amount of incumbent receipts by cycle. Then, we explore sources of variation in campaign contributions from individuals by election cycle. Finally, we assess PAC receipts by election cycle.

Total receipts

Table 2.2 reveals that the equation predicting total receipts in election cycles explains between 25 and 50 percent of the variation in total incumbent receipts across the cycle. The equations predicting middle-cycle and reelection-cycle campaign contributions are more robust than the one predicting early-cycle receipts. Consistency is evident in the patterns of monetary receipt across cycles. Incumbent Senators raise increasing amounts of the total cash in early, middle,

Table 2.2. *OLS regression estimates of total contributions to incumbent Senators, by cycle, 1978-90*

Variable	Cycle in term of office		
	Early	Middle	Reelection
	(Years 1-2)	(Years 3-4)	(Years 5-6)
Constant	-19680.28	-176227.13	1671622.23
	(-0.16)	(-0.87)	(1.96)**
Beginning of cycle — cash on hand	-0.20	0.77	0.44
	(-0.90)	(2.51)**	(0.82)
Beginning of cycle — incumbent debt	-0.02	0.001	0.72
	(-0.63)	(0.00)	(1.24)
Incumbent party	-32145.30	39832.26	-228109.74
	(-0.40)	(0.33)	(-0.46)
Former U.S. House member	-54527.62	42767.06	-144521.15
	(-0.66)	(0.35)	(-0.29)
Incumbent marginality	3286.55	-1198.24	51321.92
	(0.78)	(-0.20)	(2.10)**
Leadership	85708.30	-21767.73	971403.80
	(1.01)	(-0.19)	(2.06)**
Freshman Senator	166882.82	54659.81	201790.32
	(1.79)*	(0.40)	(0.37)
Challenger pool	33837.16	48531.14	248343.54
	(2.48)**	(2.37)**	(2.81)***
Media market diffusion index	-5.56	12.93	136.59
	(-0.46)	(0.72)	(1.81)*
Temporal counter	53973.72	24600.96	8376.31
	(3.14)***	(0.96)	(0.08)
Adjusted-R^2	.24	.34	.54
N	111	111	111

t-statistics are in parentheses.
* $p < .10$, two-tailed test.
** $p < .05$, two-tailed test.
*** $p < .01$, two-tailed test.

and election-year cycles as the pool of potential quality challengers increases. For every potential quality challenger, an incumbent Senator raises approximately $34,000 in the first third of a term and almost $50,000 per challenger in the middle third. Moreover, in the election cycle, they raise almost a quarter of a million dollars for every potential quality challenger in the pool. In addition, there is a temporally driven increase in early fund raising from 1979–80 to 1985–6.

Cash-on-hand and debt factors do not appear to be related to incumbent efforts to raise money in the first cycle of their term. Interestingly enough, however, incumbents who had large war chests at the end of the first cycle appear to increase their fund raising even more in the midterm cycle. For every dollar an incumbent has on hand, an additional seventy-seven cents typically is raised during the middle cycle. Contrary to Fenno's earlier finding, it appears that incumbents in general set about trying to prepare for reelection around the midpoint of the term. And, for those members facing large pools of challengers, who sometimes have announced their candidacies as early as three years before election (see Patterson and Kephart, 1992), fund raising becomes even more intensified. In election years, leadership status appears to provide strong benefits in terms of fund-raising potential. Marginal incumbents also appear to raise substantially more money in election-year cycles than do their more electorally secure counterparts. None of the other variables has a statistically significant impact on election-year or early fund raising.

Individual and PAC receipts

Another substantive question remains: Who is getting early money and from where do they get it? In the previous section, we noted that incumbents tend to raise more early money on average from individuals than from PACs. However, over a third of incumbents actually received more money from PACs than individuals in the early and middle cycles of their six-year term. Substantial differences exist between incumbents who raise most of their early money from PACs and those who raise their early money among individuals. Table 2.3 presents the analysis of cyclical fund raising from individuals by incumbent Senators, and the equations for cyclical receipts from PACs appear in Table 2.4. On balance, the results mirror those for total cyclical fund raising by incumbents.

The pattern of early-cycle receipts from individuals closely resembles the receipt of total money in early cycles. Senators who represent states with large pools of potential challengers raised substantial amounts of money from individual contributors during

Table 2.3. *OLS regression estimates of individual contributions to incumbent Senators, by cycle, 1978-90*

	Cycle in term of office		
	Early	Middle	Reelection
Variable	(Years 1-2)	(Years 3-4)	(Years 5-6)
Constant	-80248.63	-191709.58	765673.20
	(-0.91)	(-1.09)	(0.92)
Beginning of cycle — cash on hand	-0.16	0.50	0.09
	(-1.06)	(1.88)*	(0.16)
Beginning of cycle — incumbent debt	-0.01	-0.003	0.42
	(-0.53)	(-0.06)	(0.75)
Incumbent party	-23345.94	64084.37	-284264.65
	(0.44)	(0.62)	(0.58)
Former U.S. House member	-45497.67	16368.24	-324507.62
	(-0.85)	(0.16)	(-0.66)
Incumbent marginality	1844.23	-448.88	38960.86
	(0.68)	(-0.09)	(1.65)*
Leadership	11434.44	-15253.06	852922.40
	(0.23)	(-0.15)	(1.86)*
Freshman Senator	94020.73	32847.98	188000.13
	(1.55)	(0.28)	(0.35)
Challenger pool	18908.74	39120.35	249905.20
	(2.14)**	(2.20)**	(2.90)***
Media market diffusion index	0.80	10.79	96.90
	(0.10)	(0.70)	(0.35)
Temporal counter	30588.16	23335.77	769.98
	(2.75)***	(1.05)	(0.01)
Adjusted-R^2	.23	.29	.46
N	111	111	111

t-statistics are in parentheses.
* $p < .10$, two-tailed test.
** $p < .05$, two-tailed test.
*** $p < .01$, two-tailed test.

the first two years of their term. Senators increased the amount of money raised from individual donors in general throughout the 1980s. No other predictors were statistically significant.

Middle-cycle receipts of campaign contributions from individuals appear to be driven largely by the size of the opposition candidate pool. Much like the results for our analysis of total receipts, incum-

Table 2.4. *OLS regression estimates of PAC contributions to incumbent Senators, by cycle, 1978-90*

| | Cycle in term of office | | |
| | Early | Middle | Reelection |
Variable	(Years 1-2)	(Years 3-4)	(Years 5-6)
Constant	12732.30	34438.68	715587.79
	(0.59)	(1.09)	(5.29)***
Beginning of cycle — cash on hand	-0.09	0.03	0.15
	(-2.60)***	(0.68)	(1.80)*
Beginning of cycle — incumbent debt	-0.0003	0.0004	0.15
	(-0.04)	(0.05)	(1.68)*
Incumbent party	-7881.27	-14130.32	52079.81
	(-0.62)	(-0.76)	(0.66)
Former U.S. House member	-5187.82	30056.93	203725.81
	(-0.40)	(1.59)	(2.54)**
Incumbent marginality	844.78	240.52	9404.13
	(1.28)	(0.26)	(2.43)**
Leadership	3690.63	-10668.92	68076.06
	(0.30)	(-0.60)	(0.91)
Freshman Senator	35838.80	-16141.86	9640.75
	(2.44)**	(-0.76)	(0.11)
Challenger pool	2387.60	5321.49	-1406.76
	(1.11)	(1.66)*	(-0.10)
Media market diffusion index	1.70	2.10	28.77
	(0.89)	(0.75)	(2.40)*
Temporal counter	5313.83	3483.83	20471.44
	(1.97)**	(0.87)	(1.26)
Adjusted-R^2	.27	.19	.35
N	111	111	111

t-statistics are in parentheses.
 * $p < .10$, two-tailed test.
 ** $p < .05$, two-tailed test.
 *** $p < .01$, two-tailed test.

bents apparently intensified their midterm fund raising among individuals as the pool of potential challengers they might encounter grew larger. This trend continues to be evident in fund raising among individuals during the election-year cycle.

The results of the analysis of cyclical receipts from PACs diverge substantially from the results of either the total receipts or the receipts from individuals analyses. Incumbent Senators are more likely to receive substantial receipts from PACs if they are freshman Senators. New Senators typically raised approximately $36,000 more in the first two years of a term from PACs than did more senior incumbents. A relationship between cash reserves and fund raising from PACs is also evident. As Fenno (1982) hypothesized, incumbents attempt to replenish diminished war chests from PAC sources. For every dollar of cash on hand an incumbent possesses, PAC receipts diminish by nine cents. This suggests that PACs either target, or are solicited by, incumbents who depleted their cash stocks in pursuit of election or reelection. A significant temporal trend is detected, indicating that campaign contributions acquired during the early-cycle receipts have increased over time. None of the predictors of campaign receipts were significantly related to capturing PAC money at midterm, although two variables appear to be modestly related to getting PAC money at midterm: the challenger pool size and whether a Senator is a former House member.

There is an interesting shift in the receipt of PAC monies by incumbents in their re-election year. Political action committees contribute more money to electorally vulnerable incumbents. This suggests PACs are generally responsive to the election-year needs of vulnerable Senators. They also give large amounts of money to incumbents who represent large states, especially those with several very large media markets. Political action committees appear to be particularly responsive to incumbent Senators who previously served in the U.S. House. Former House members raise over $200,000 more than other Senators from PACs. Limits to candidate connections in fund raising are evident, although they are less constraining for Senators who are former House members.

The results of our analyses indicate that there are fundamental differences in the fund-raising approaches of Senators. Incumbents who are electorally vulnerable tend to concentrate on fund raising among individuals during the first four years of the electoral term. Only in the election years do PACs begin to make substantial contributions to vulnerable incumbents. This possibly reflects the desire of PACs to invest their resources when the need for cash by vulnerable incumbents becomes most acute. By following such a strategy, the potential rewards for timely assistance are enhanced. Political action committees also appear to be most willing to respond early in the Senator's term to replenish the depleted cash reserves of incumbents. Despite the relatively low influence they bring relative to the leadership, freshman Senators appear to enjoy very profitable relationships with PACs early in their first term. Former House members appear to be best positioned to extract substantial money from PAC sources, although this difference is only apparent in election-year cycles.

The emphasis on early fund raising among individuals by incumbents who face large challenger pools may be a by-product of the contacting and campaigning necessary in representing large states or states where potential opponents are numerous. If these Senators are "running scared," they are simply emulating the behavior of House members. If so, tremendous effort is expended attempting to build or maintain constituency networks, raise funds from prominent in-state sources, and deter challengers (Fenno, 1991a). Incumbent members are not just building war chests, but also a network of support that might be perceived to preempt the strongest potential challengers.

Evidence of efficient rent acquisition

To test empirically the actual efficiency of Senators in profit taking through their campaign contributions, we define rents as financial support contributed to Senators by third parties rather than loans provided by an incumbent to one's own campaign. Three principle sources exist from which Senators may capture profits: individuals, PACs, and party committees (see Stanley and Niemi, 1992; Herrnson, 1989; Sorauf, 1988). We do not include independent or "on-behalf" expenditures as captured rents.[5] Although these monies may enhance the ability of legislators to maintain their seats or facilitate their rent-seeking activities, they are neither convertible nor accessible for long-term direct use, except to support reelection in the current cycle. Moreover, by limiting rent sources to party, PAC, and individual campaign contributions, we account for the overwhelming majority of financial support obtained by Senate incumbents throughout the 1980s (Jacobson, 1989). Because each of these types of contributions represents a nonobligatory financial resource that does not require cash repayment, they may be viewed as potential sources of revenue from which profits can be extracted. Rents, then, are specified as

$$R = C_i + C_{PAC} + C_p \qquad [2]$$

where: R = total revenue; C_i = contributions by individuals; C_{PAC} = contributions by PACs; and C_p = contributions by parties, respectively, in the election cycle.

The mere receipt of campaign contributions as revenue, however, does not necessarily indicate that incumbents are successfully engaged in an efficient, profitable enterprise. Are Senators able to preserve some of their campaign receipts and likewise retain their Senate seat? If not, the exercise in which they engaged is not necessarily an efficient one. In order to identify the efficient rent seekers among Senate incumbents, we subtract campaign expenditures and outstanding debts owed by the incumbent after the general election from the revenue obtained in equation [2] in order to obtain net rents:

$$R' = R - (D_t + E_{rs}) \qquad [3]$$

where: R' = net revenue; D_t = debts at the end of the campaign at time t; and E_{rs} = expenditures by the campaign in the election-year cycle to maintain the seat. Candidates for whom R' is greater than 0 have succeeded in efficient profit taking, although the dollar value of the residual rents may be very small in some cases. Those incumbents for whom R' is less than 0 have fully dissipated their revenue and incurred debt in order to retain their policy-entrepreneur position. These legislators are likely to continue to engage in rent-seeking behavior by virtue of their position to provide selective benefits to monied interests and because of the financial losses incurred in the campaign that they will seek to externalize (Paul and Wilhite, 1990; Denzau and Munger, 1986).

Variation in efficient rent acquisition

Data on the monetary value of campaign contributions were obtained from reports filed by each incumbent Senator with the Federal Election Commission (FEC) from 1977 through 1990. This produces a total of 111 contests for Senate seats involving incumbents who chose to seek reelection during the 1984 through 1990 election cycles. The analysis gives a view of incumbents' behavior over a sufficient period of time to note patterns and trends in that behavior. In order to control for the effect of inflation on the monetary value of profits received, all financial data are expressed as constant 1990 dollars.

Based on our criterion for efficient profit taking outlined above, 45 of the 111 incumbents succeeded in protecting at least part of the financial largesse they acquired during their reelection campaigns. The largest rents were retained by then-Senate Majority Leader Robert Dole in 1986: $998,945.10. Although GOP leader Dole was the most efficient profit-maker, 11 of the top 14 (and 13 of the top 20) in efficiency were Democrats.[6] The roll call of Senators who were particularly adept at running a surplus includes such notables as John Glenn (1990, $783,000), Sam Nunn (1990, $906,440), Ted Kennedy (1988, $559,583), Al Gore (1990, $486,878), and Dan Quayle (1986, $292,851). The least amount of money retained by an efficient profit seeker was just $884 by New Hampshire's Warren Rudman, in 1986. Rudman raised just over $1.2 million, and almost 97 percent of his support was obtained from individual donors; he spent just under $1.2 million. As coauthor of Gramm-Rudman-Hollings, Rudman may have been demonstrating characteristic Yankee frugality by only raising sufficient funds to insure reelection without incurring debt or by trying to demonstrate symbolically the efficacy of a balanced budget with his own campaign![7] The least efficient profit seeker was Frank Lautenburg in 1988 (−$5.5 million).[8] Among nonmillionaires, Alphonse D'Amato and Pete Wilson each spent over $2 million in excess of revenue to maintain their seats.

Table 2.5 reveals there has been no appreciable increase in the number of efficient profit seekers over time. However, there was a noticeable decline in efficient profit seekers during the 1985–6 and 1987–8 election cycles followed by a tremendous rebound in 1990. Why, then, is there volatility in efficient profit seeking by incumbents during the 1980s, especially among Republicans? Evidence from several sources of campaign funding suggest possible bases for such volatility. Figure 2.2 indicated that a substantial increase in early (non-reelection-cycle) fund raising occurred between 1980 and 1988,

Table 2.5. *Frequency of efficient profit taking by incumbent Senators, 1984-90*

| | Cycle | | | | |
	1983-84	1985-86	1987-88	1989-90	Total
All Senators					
Inefficient	15	16	20	15	66 (59.5)
Efficient	14	11	5	15	45 (40.5)
N	29	27	25	30	111
Democrats					
Inefficient	6	4	10	9	29 (56.9)
Efficient	6	5	4	7	22 (43.1)
N	12	9	14	16	51
Republicans					
Inefficient	9	12	10	6	37 (61.7)
Efficient	8	6	1	8	23 (38.3)
N	17	18	11	14	60

Numbers in parentheses are percentages.

and in Table 2.1 we observed an overall growth in mean PAC receipts to incumbent Senators of both parties. Mean PAC contributions peaked for both parties in 1988, the same election cycle when efficient profit seeking reaches its nadir. Table 2.1 also revealed that overall donations from individuals increased for Democratic incumbents over time, converging in 1990 to exceed the mean level of contributions made to GOP incumbents.

It is plausible that the decline in efficient profit taking during the late 1980s stems from stronger challengers confronting incumbents. Mean receipts by Democratic challengers increased through 1988 before falling precipitously in 1990. Mean spending by GOP challengers, by comparison, peaked in 1986 before exhibiting a slight drop in 1988. During this period, efficient profit takers declined from 47.1 percent of Republicans pursuing reelection in 1984 to 33.3 percent in 1986 to just 9.1 percent in 1988. Efficient profit seeking by Democrats holding Senate seats did not diminish as dramatically, although the percentage of efficient profit seekers among Democratic incumbents in 1988 (28.6%) was far below their rates for the 1984 (50.0%), 1986 (55.6%), and 1990 (43.8%) elections.

Republican efforts in unsuccessfully defending several seats in 1986 substantially diminished efficiency in campaigning in that year.

The impact of the tremendous seat swing against Republican incumbents in 1986 may have persuaded incumbent Republican Senators to increase spending in the 1988 elections just to maintain their seats and then to attempt to realize profits at some future date.

Multivariate analysis

As the preceding discussion indicates, a variety of factors may affect the ability of incumbent Senators to acquire and preserve their financial resources. An array of institutional and individual factors may affect monetary exchanges between contributors and Senators seeking reelection. Although existing research reveals little impact attributable to marginality on election outcomes (see Bernstein, 1989), the relative electoral vulnerability of Senators may well influence contribution strategies, as well as Senators' contribution-seeking activities (see Regens, Gaddie, and Elliott, 1994, 1993). Senate incumbents whose prior margin of victory suggests they are relatively "safe" from strong challenges may be able to extract larger profits since they are not likely to be replaced by a successor and face lower reelection costs (Parker, 1992a). The leadership continues to play a major agenda-setting role. Accordingly, although leadership positions were not associated with early rent acquisition, being in a leadership position may be associated with receiving substantial profits.

Reflecting advancement patterns in terms of the relative prestige of electoral offices, a number of incumbent Senators (25.2%) have prior service as a member of the House of Representatives. Among those Senators seeking reelection during the series of cycles from 1984 to 1990, 15.6 percent moved directly from the House to the Senate in 1978 or later. In the previous analysis of early fund raising, we noted that former House members obtained substantially more PAC money than other incumbents. These Senators may have carried their continual electioneering and fund-raising habits into the Senate (Mayhew, 1974). Those Senators may also be more adept at the fund-raising and allocation decisions necessary to more efficiently retain rents.

Attributes of Senate challengers also may impact on incumbents' ability to capture campaign contributions from individual donors,

PACs, and their own party. Previous research indicates that highly experienced challengers are adept at raising funds (Squire, 1991). That ability may also selectively impair the ability of incumbents to capture substantial contributions from some resources. For example, incumbent receipts from corporate PACs decline as those PACs allocate more money to potentially viable challengers (Regens, Gaddie, and Elliott, 1994, 1993). Alternatively, PACs and parties may attempt to aid incumbents who face well-financed challengers. To test whether these assumptions hold for the overall monetary support retained by incumbents, we include the amount of dollars expended by an incumbent's general election opponent as a financial measure of challenger financial quality (Abramowitz, 1989).

Although the percentage of funds raised that are retained may not be as great as for members from smaller states, Senators from larger states may be able to leverage the need to cover more diffuse media markets into larger net profits (see Nagler and Leighley, 1992; Squire, 1991). The ability of Senators to externalize campaign costs in their rent-seeking activities should be more evident as those costs increase and therefore become less certain. The media-market index introduced in the cyclical fund-raising analysis is designed to reflect the size of a state media market as well as the dispersion of that media among multiple centers (see also Campbell, Alford, and Henry, 1984).

Although Squire (1991) has indicated that preemptive spending does not have a direct impact on challenger profiles, increases in cash on hand indicates early profit seeking and therefore may be related to efficiency in profit retention. Squire (1991), asserts that the quality of emerging challengers in Senate elections is unrelated to war-chest building or preemptive spending. As a result, incumbents who build strong war chests early may expect tougher campaigns or may be attempting to capture their profits early and offset future costs.

The specific sources from which incumbents acquire campaign contributions also may affect the magnitude of retained funds. Candidates who obtain large amounts of money from individuals may not expect particularly difficult reelection campaigns. Alternatively, they may have a broader base of support typical of a safe incumbent (see also Fenno, 1978; Matthews, 1960). By comparison, candidates who obtain excessive funding from particularized interests – groups with potentially focused expectations of selective benefits from their investment – may be more vulnerable and therefore less capable of retaining campaign funds as profits. Party funding may be channeled to incumbents in danger of losing their seat, although limitations on party money constrain substantial, direct contributions to candidates (Jacobson, 1989). In addition to these theoretically plausible variables, because we examine efficient profit seeking across multiple election cycles, we control for temporal impacts.

We test our assumptions with the following OLS equation:

$$Y = a + b_1X_1 + b_2X_2 + b_3X_3 + b_4X_4 + b_5X_5 + b_6X_6$$
$$+ b_7X_7 + b_8X_8 + b_9X_9 + b_{10}X_{10} + e \qquad [4]$$

where:

$Y =$ net profits (R$'$)

$X_1 =$ dummy variable coded 1 for any member in committee leadership positions (committee chair, ranking member), 2 for members of the floor leadership (see Parker, 1992a), and 0 otherwise

$X_2 =$ margin of previous reelection victory, defined as 50 percent minus the candidate's total percentage of the two-party vote

$X_3 =$ dummy variable coded 1 for any member who previously served in the House of Representatives, and 0 otherwise

$X_4 =$ incumbent cash on hand at the beginning of the reelection cycle $(t - 1)$, expressed in constant 1990 dollars

$X_5 =$ party contributions to the candidate, in constant 1990 dollars

$X_6 =$ PAC contributions to the candidate, in constant 1990 dollars.

$X_7 =$ contributions by individuals to the candidate, in constant 1990 dollars

$X_8 =$ Media-market dispersion index, calculated by multiplying the number of TV households in a state (in thousands) by the dispersal of TV households among local markets

$X_9 =$ challenger spending, expressed in constant 1990 dollars

$X_{10} =$ a continuous counter ranging from 1 to 4, pegged to 1 and increasing by 1 with each election cycle from 1984 to 1990.

Results

The results of the OLS estimates in Table 2.6 indicate a fairly robust fit between our regression equation and efficient profit taking (adjusted-R^2 = 0.50), and confirm a number of our assumptions about efficient profit taking. Incumbents who served in the House prior to being elected to the Senate are likely to retain substantial amounts of campaign contributions once an election cycle is completed. Prior House experience makes it likely that these Senators will retain over $350,000 more than their colleagues lacking comparable service in the lower chamber. This supports our assumption that former House members serving in the Senate continue to retain some of the behavioral characteristics of their previous service in the lower chamber, especially the ability to retain campaign contributions across election cycles.

Senators who raise large sums of money from individual donors also are more likely to retain campaign contributions than are those who raise large sums of money from PACs. In fact, Senate incumbents who rely heavily upon PAC money tend to be relatively inefficient in their efforts to retain those funds as profits. PACs direct more aid to incumbents who face more difficult, costly reelections or are responding to incumbents who have turned to PAC sources to shore up campaigns with immediate vulnerability problems. If this is the case, substantial PAC resources are used to defray costs, rather than enhance profits. Although individual contributions and PAC allocations both influence efficient profit taking, party money provided to aid Senate incumbents in their quest for reelection exerts a trivial impact on efficient rent seeking. The lack of statistical significance for party money reflects the limits on direct party contributions enforced by the FEC under the Federal Elections Campaign Act.

Challenger spending is strongly related to the ability of incumbents to preserve surplus campaign funds as profits. As Abramowitz (1989) observed, Senate challenger success increases with spending (see also Squire, 1989). This leads us to speculate that incumbents facing well-financed challengers are likely to spend more of their campaign funds (i.e., dissipate potential profits) in an attempt to protect their

Table 2.6. *OLS estimate of efficient profit taking by incumbent Senators, 1984-90*

Variable	Unstandardized coefficient
Constant	-1044.53
Cash on hand (*t*-1)	-0.74
	(-5.24)***
Former U.S. House member	371757.40
	(2.83)***
Incumbent marginality	-7402.49
	(-1.22)
Leadership	106300.84
	(1.02)
Media market diffusion index	23.12
	(1.67)*
Temporal counter	45345.50
	(1.85)*
Party contributions	2.18
	(0.43)
PAC contributions	-0.36
	(-2.21)**
Contributions from individuals	0.06
	(1.80)*
Challenger spending	-0.20
	(-5.28)***
Adjusted-R^2	.50
N	111

Dependent variable is the net profits obtained by some senator (R'; see equation [3.3] in this chapter).
t-statistics are in parentheses.
* $p < .10$, two-tailed test.
** $p < .05$, two-tailed test.
*** $p < .01$, two-tailed test.

seats. This interpretation is consistent with the hypothesized relationship between increased challenger spending and reduced profit-taking efficiency by incumbent Senators.

Media-market size and the degree of decentralization are also positively related to the retention of substantial profits. This underscores the ability of incumbents running in states with several major media markets to retain a larger surplus of campaign funds at the end of a campaign than their counterparts running in states with a limited number of TV households or media markets. Interestingly enough, the potentially higher costs for media in bigger states works to an incumbent's advantage in terms of keeping campaign contributions as profits. The temporal counter reveals the efficiency of incumbents in retaining campaign contributions increased during the 1980s (see also Stanley and Niemi, 1992:182–3). Leadership and marginality were not significant influences on efficient profit taking, although the signs for those coefficients were in the hypothesized directions.

The impact of rent-seeking Senators

Incumbents Senators demonstrate a remarkable propensity for garnering excess profits from their positions in the policy hierarchy. The magnitude of these rents is dependent on a variety of incumbent attributes, as well as on the sources from which incumbents build their war chests. The extent to which incumbents rely on individual donors or PAC money, whether incumbents have prior service as a House member, the size and decentralization of state media markets, and the financial resources of an incumbent's opponent are all strongly related to the ability of Senate incumbents to retain substantial amounts of financial largesse. Factors significantly related to the receipt of contributions – such as marginality and being a member of the chamber's leadership – are not related to the ability of Senate incumbents to extract profits from their campaigns. In essence, although incumbents are capable of raising excessive funds, they are not necessarily able to retain substantial net surpluses. That the members of the Senate who often retained the most substantial profits from their campaigns were former members of the U.S. House indicates that the excessive fund-raising proclivities that dominate behavior of incumbent Representatives are carried with them as they move into the Senate (see Fenno, 1982).

Incumbents who rely less on PAC money than on individual contributions are retaining more of their war chest after the election. These incumbents are probably less in need of the quick infusions of cash that PACs can provide. As a result, they have less need to raise funds outside of the network of individual supporters they have cultivated during their tenure. The campaign contributions provided by organized interests, therefore, assume the attributes of a gift. As gifts, these contributions carry relatively low repayment obligations for the recipients. As a result, the campaign-finance system constitutes a quasi market that provides incumbent Senators with ample incentive and opportunities to extract substantial financial support from particularized interests in return for the provision of policy outputs (Grier, Munger, and Torrent, 1991; Denzau and Munger, 1986). The financial largesse these Senators collect exceeds their electoral needs in many cases. It is surprising that the construction of large war chests prior to the reelection cycle does not contribute to the efficiency of the reelection campaign. All the effort expended seeking and acquiring early money is to maintain the policy position. Members who engage in rent-seeking activity and spend the greatest effort seeking reelection sacrifice their rents and their time in Washington. The vulnerability of many Senators inevitably leads to engaging in rent-seeking behavior, although the only long-term reward is the policy position.

For other incumbents, however, the ability to extract substantial revenue from the campaign-finance system does not indicate an ability to retain those funds after the election. Incumbents who raise more substantial amounts of PAC money rely on such support to maintain their position in the policy hierarchy, while externalizing the costs of doing so (Paul and Wilhite, 1990). They are not able to extract additional benefits from their financial support. Financially vulnerable incumbents constitute more profitable, albeit risky, investments for PACs, because the value of every contribution to the success of that incumbent's reelection effort is greater than for incumbents who run more efficient campaigns (Regens, Gaddie, and Elliott, 1994, 1993).

Viewing the exchanges in the campaign-finance system as a market for profit-seeking enterprise enhances our understanding of possible inefficiencies in the campaign-finance system. Senators are positioned to provide selective benefits to interested parties and acquire additional direct benefits for themselves. The ability of members to efficiently conduct campaigns within the constraints of funds raised is limited, however, thereby limiting the number of incumbents who can successfully extract positive benefits from their campaign-finance efforts. Ironically, those incumbents who often extract the greatest support from organized interests are the same Senators who are least able to derive nonelectoral benefits from their efforts. That excessive incumbent spending at the margins is highly reactive to challenger spending reinforces the necessity of vulnerable Senators to sell policy outputs. The dependence of Senators on the policy market to maintain their position at the cost of discretion and their acquired rents indicates that the pursuit of political office is a largely inefficient pursuit.

3. Targeting rent provision by major interests

> A landed interest, a manufacturing interest, a mercantile interest, a mon-
> eyed interest, with many lesser interests, [which] grow up of necessity in
> civilized nations and divide them into different classes, actuated by dif-
> ferent sentiments and views.
>
> James Madison
> *Federalist, Number 10*

The previous chapter demonstrated the encroachment of rent-seeking behavior throughout the Senate term and identified indicators of efficiency in rent seeking by Senators. In this chapter, we analyze the allocations of economic interests to incumbent Senators through political-action-committee (PAC) contributions. In particular, we are concerned with identifying the sources from which Senators obtain their rents and identifying the criteria by which PACs allocate campaign contributions as variable benefits.

Rent provision by economic interests

In order to examine the subtleties of the relationships between legislators and organized interests in the context of rent seeking, it is important to delineate the constraints and facilities that will affect a legislator's ability to garner rents. Presumably, organized interests seek the lowest-cost, highest-yield providers of policy options. The degree to which a legislator can provide sufficient policy to an interest at a competitive price with other members of the policy oligopoly will dictate the amount of rents the legislator will obtain in the aggregate. Therefore, member attributes that affect the costs of providing different types of policy should influence the decision by cash-providing interests to provide substantial rents to that member.

Other factors impact on the ability of legislators to provide policy outputs to benefit-seeking interests. The size of rents are determined by the marginal cost to the member of providing policy. Members who have lower marginal costs of policy production will therefore attract more contributions in the aggregate and also garner more total rents. The ability of the legislator to guide policy initiatives through legislative channels such as committee markup, floor debate, coalition building, or even by using delaying tactics such as the filibuster should therefore impact rent acquisition.

The constituency concerns of the legislators will also influence their cost of policy provision. Legislators who are concerned with reelection will incorporate salient constituency concerns into policy decisions. If the provision of policy P will somehow impact adversely on the legislator's reelection constituency, then the cost of providing some policy P will likewise increase. As a result, the amount of rents accrued from providing policy P necessarily will be diminished. The electoral vulnerability of an incumbent also may affect the decision to provide a policy output. Presumably, legislators who view themselves as electorally secure may be willing to absorb a certain amount of "goodwill" cost vis-à-vis their constituency in order to obtain a rent. Or, members may feel sufficiently secure that they will exercise discretion in order to garner rents. Alternatively, vulnerable legislators may be willing to lower the cost of policy provision in exchange for rents, regardless of constituency considerations. If the reelection constituency is considered tenuous at best, a legislator may lower the policy-provision price to attract interest-group support. For those Senators, additional losses of goodwill may not be important if the net effect is an increase in their war chest. Senators who sacrifice goodwill for rents will likely enjoy a reduced level of discretion, because they are constrained by the expectation of a tenuous reelection constituency *and* by the policy commitments made in exchange for financial support. This potential mode of behavior reflects the assumption that the rents accrued will adequately offset any costs in terms of constituency support. Finally, incumbents are likely to engage in extensive rent seeking from interests, then dissipate those rents to retain their policy oligopoly position (Paul and Wilhite,

1990). Under this scenario, any efficient rent seeking will need to be left to the future.

Legislator attributes

Partisan politics and an incumbent's ideology should play an important role in shaping rent-seeking outcomes (Evans, 1988; Poole, Romer, and Rosenthal, 1987; Eismeier and Pollack, 1986a; Gopoian, 1984). For instance, partisan control of the Congress may help shape regulatory outcomes since Democratic and Republican elites appear to diverge substantially in their support for command-and-control versus market-based incentives for regulation (Regens, 1989; McCubbins and Page, 1985; McCubbins, 1985). Regulatory decisions, their broader societal merits notwithstanding, can have major impacts on the relative equilibrium of the distribution of benefits and costs across society. In fact, in the complex world of regulatory policy making, where government involvement in market processes is pervasive, legislators possess significant capability to influence policy content and consequences (see Regens and Elliott, 1992; Grier, Munger, and Torrent, 1990; Wood, 1990; Regens, 1989; Harris and Milkis, 1989).

The ideological orientation of incumbents may have bearing on their receipts from various financial sources. Among corporate PACs, for instance, fairly sophisticated contribution patterns have been observed. This certainly is suggestive that ideology, as reflected in roll-call voting, is related to financial support (Regens, Gaddie, and Elliott, 1994; Parker, 1992a). These influences are also evident among other types of PACs (Grier and Munger, 1991).[1]

Seniority also may affect the level of one's PAC contributions (see Poole and Romer, 1985). Legislators who have retained their seats for a number of years may exercise substantial influence based on well-established relationships with fellow Senators as well as with other Washington actors who may influence policy creation. The dramatic increase in freshman participation, coupled with the dramatic turnover in chamber membership since 1976 has diminished the role of seniority in debate, sponsorship, and other legislative activity. The analysis presented in Chapter 2 revealed that freshmen are attractive investments for PACs in the aggregate. This underscores the need to test whether the costs of participating in the policy making for junior legislators have lowered to the point that seniority is tremendously discounted as an asset when seeking rents.

Electoral and constituency factors

Little empirical support exists for the hypothesis that marginality produces greater direct responsiveness to constituency interests (see Bernstein, 1989). Nonetheless, it is worthwhile to explore whether the relative electoral vulnerability of Senators impacts on differentials in corporate giving. In the case of campaign finance, it is possible that electoral marginality may influence allocation strategies, with those Senators believed to be electorally vulnerable being more likely to attract excess contributions.[2] Such an outcome might stem from increased efforts by those Senators to attract funds as well as the likelihood that PACs would view them as productive, albeit uncertain, investments.

Incumbents often measure their vulnerability in terms of how they performed during the previous election. Because they value their seats, any close call or perceived vulnerability may lead to increased campaigning and quasi-campaigning activity in order to hold their seat (Mayhew, 1974). This can include increased constituency service, mailings, district visits, and of course fund raising (Fiorina, 1989; Ferejohn, 1977). Although Fenno (1978) and Squire (1989) have noted that virtually all incumbents "run scared" regardless of actual safety, differences in the allocations of monies by PACs may depend on the electoral vulnerability of the incumbent (Grier and Munger, 1991). Parker (1992b) attributes this phenomenon to the desire of politicians to maximize their discretion in Washington. Legislators seek an optimal vote share that insures their electoral safety but does not necessarily maximize the potential share of the vote. To maximize votes would require an expenditure of effort that might encroach on the exercise of discretion in Washington.

Incumbents who won marginal victories in their last reelection effort may be particularly disposed to obtaining large amounts of money for their next campaign. Because electorally vulnerable incumbents perceive the need to increase their safety, they will raise additional money to scare off potential opponents (Squire, 1991; Green and Krasno, 1988). Political action committees in general are inclined to direct money to vulnerable incumbents due to their needs. These incumbents may be willing to provide benefits for a lower cost than a safe incumbent, who may try to extract a larger contribution, and this may make them attractive to particularized interests (Denzau and Munger, 1986).[3]

Incumbents who face highly experienced opponents may be the beneficiaries of substantial financial support. This follows for several reasons. First, politically experienced challengers are more common in Senate races than in House races (Squire, 1989). Challengers with greater political experience are more adept at raising campaign funds (Green and Krasno, 1988). This may encourage PACs to aid sympathetic incumbents who face strong challengers, in an attempt to offset the fund-raising skill of a strong challenger (Regens, Elliott, and Gaddie, 1994). To capture these effects, we utilize a measure of challenger quality. Our indicator is coded on a scale of 0 to 8, based upon the criteria specified by Green and Krasno (1988) and it captures both political and celebrity attributes that enhance a challenger's political strength.[4]

It is also conceivable that the amount of money contributed by a PAC cohort to an incumbent's opponent in the general election is likely to influence the level of rents an incumbent receives. Presumably, as contributions to the challenger measured in constant 1990 dollars increase, the probability of successfully acquiring substantial rents decreases. In essence, self-interest may induce PACs to hedge their bets. They can attempt to do so by selectively funding challengers as well as incumbents in contested Senate elections. Of course, interest groups and individual donors may engage in bet-covering contribution strategies that support both incumbents and challengers, although evidence from corporate PAC behavior does not support this proposition in U.S. Senate elections (Regens, Gaddie, and Elliott, 1994, 1993).

In addition to these theoretically plausible variables, it is reasonable to test whether an increase in acquiring substantial contributions happens over time. In Chapter 2, we noted the long-term growth in PAC contributions across a variety of sources. In a multivariate analysis, this can be represented by the coefficient associated with a continuous counter indicating each election cycle from 1982 to 1988. Because the 1984 and 1988 Senate elections were concurrent with presidential elections, the greater visibility and intensity of campaigning in presidential election years may foster enhanced rent seeking by incumbents. Alternatively, PAC managers may increase their contributions if they perceive presidential elections entail greater risks for preferred Senators who are members of the disadvantaged party. For example, in 1984 and 1988 corporate PACs may have selectively provided additional campaign funds to specific Democratic Senators to help them overcome the problems associated with relatively weak Democratic presidential nominees at the top of their ticket (Eismeier and Pollock, 1986b).

Committee jurisdictions

One empirically validated hypothesis of PAC behavior is that particular interests are able to target financial support to members of committees directly affecting the interest's regulatory environment (Parker, 1992a; Grier and Munger, 1991; Regens, Elliott, and Gaddie, 1991; Munger, 1989; Denzau and Munger, 1986). Munger (1989) finds corporate PACs allocate funds disproportionately to members of those committees maintaining jurisdiction over policy areas salient to a particular industry (see also Regens, Gaddie, and Elliott, 1994, 1993; Regens, Elliott, and Gaddie, 1991; Grier and Munger, 1991). Such findings are consistent with the importance attributed to the congressional committee system and its jurisdictional prerogatives (see Parker and Parker, 1979).

To test whether such an impact holds for rent provision, we include controls for membership on six legislative committees that hold the primary tax-writing, or oversight, functions for corporate, trade, labor, and cooperative PACs (Grier and Munger, 1991; Parker, 1992a). Those committees, and the interests to which they are most important (in parentheses), are: Labor (labor PACs); Banking (corporate PACs, trade PACs); Energy and Natural Resources (corporate PACs, trade PACs); Commerce, Science and Technology (corporate PACs and trade PACs); Agriculture (cooperative PACs, and possibly corporate PACs); and Small Business (corporate PACs and trade PACs). On the other hand, Senators typically have multiple committee assignments, and Grier, Munger, and Torrent (1990) find committee influence to be greatly diminished in the Senate when interests make allocation decisions. This may reduce the incentives for individual Senators to develop the kind of policy specialization encouraged in the House because Senators can gain prominence that is independent of their committee assignments by participating in a broad range of policy decisions (Sinclair, 1989). Institutional changes within the Congress also have weakened norms of committee specialization and reciprocity which may lead interests to decrease emphasis on committee influence or expertise (see Grier, Munger, and Torrent, 1990; Sinclair, 1989). To determine whether Senators serving on committees identified as important to those clusters of PACs receive significantly greater contributions than other members from that set of PACs, we include a series of controls for committee assignment.

In addition to these theoretically plausible variables, there is the possibility that temporal effects unrelated to inflation or changes in incumbent attributes are at work, which have increased the level of giving. Therefore, we use the temporal counter specified in the models for Chapter 2 to control for these effects.

Campaign-finance data, including expenditure information, were obtained from the Federal Elections Commission (FEC) releases of campaign-finance reports through the Inter-University Consortium for Political and Social Research at the University of Michigan.[5] These financial reports indicate the level of support received by Senate individual candidates from several sources. All financial data were converted to 1990 dollars to control for inflation.

The equation to test for variation in financial support to incumbents by corporate, trade, labor, and cooperative PACs is specified as

$$Y_i = a + b_1X_1 + b_2X_2 + b_3X_3 + b_4X_4 + b_5X_5 + b_6X_6 + b_7X_7 + b_8X_8 + b_9X_9 + b_{10}X_{10} + b_{11}X_{11} + b_{12}X_{12} + e \qquad [5]$$

where

Y_i = dollars to the incumbent from some PAC_i-cohort (corporate, labor, trade or cooperative)

Table 3.1. *Summary statistics of PAC contributions to Senate incumbents from 1982-88, expressed in constant 1990 dollars*

	PAC Cohort			
	Corporate	Labor	Trade	Cooperative
Mean contribution	429,659	112,526	224,197	15,525
S_d	279,869	116,532	105,742	16,349
Minimum	0	0	0	0
Maximum	1,555,507	380,177	572,787	66,921
Total contributions	48,121,871	12,602,959	25,110,148	1,738,847
Percentage of all economic PAC contributions	54.95	14.39	28.67	1.99
N = 112				

X_1 = incumbent ideology, measured by the National Journal Composite Score

X_2 = incumbent seniority

X_3 = incumbent marginality

X_4 = challenger experience

X_5 = party (1 = Democrat)

X_6 = temporal counter

X_7 = Labor Committee

X_8 = Banking Committee

X_9 = Energy and Natural Resources Committee

X_{10} = Agriculture Committee

X_{11} = Small Business Committee

X_{12} = Commerce, Science, and Technology Committee

e = error term.

Patterns of PAC allocations

The aggregate contributions from corporate, trade, labor, and cooperative PACs to Senators appear in Table 3.1. Total receipts by Senators from these PACs were a staggering $87.4 million from 1982 to 1988 (expressed in constant 1990 dollars). Of those receipts, 54.95 percent came from corporate sources and 28.67 percent from trade-association PACs, indicating that almost 85 percent of Senators' PAC contributions were obtained from private-sector and professional interests. Labor PACs, on the other hand, gave only 14.39 percent of all PAC contributions to incumbent Senators, whereas co-operative PACs accounted for a minuscule 1.99 percent of PAC contributions. Moreover, substantial variation in PAC giving exists when controls for party affiliation are introduced. Corporate sources gave twice as much money to Republicans as to Democrats from 1982 to 1988, whereas trade PACs split their contributions to incumbents approximately 55:45 in favor of Republicans. Consistent with the long-standing links to the Democratic Party, labor gave six times as much support to Democratic Senators as to Republicans.

Corporate PACs

The results of the regression analysis for corporate PAC contributions appear in Table 3.2. Corporate PACs appear to engage in a sophisticated contribution strategy that rewards Republicans and ideological conservatives regardless of party label. These PACs also fund Senate candidates who face tough challengers or have higher aggregate campaign expenses due to constituency size.

Throughout the 1980s, Democrats obtain significantly less money than Republicans from corporate PACs. In fact, the regression coefficient for party identification indicates that a typical Senate Democrat received approximately $165,000 less than a Republican colleague. Not surprisingly, regardless of party, conservatives benefit in terms of campaign contributions from corporations. To illustrate this, consider that a Senator whose score is at the median in terms of ideology (50) will receive approximately $190,000 more than the most liberal member of the Senate.[6]

Corporate allocations also reflect the personal electoral needs of potentially vulnerable incumbents. Senators who face higher-quality, more-experienced challengers receive substantially greater corporate PAC support. For example, a Senator facing an incumbent governor

Table 3.2. *Corporate PAC contributions*

Variable	Unstandardized Coefficient	t-statistic
Constant	44678.87	
Challenger quality	26324.70	3.06***
Democrat	-164234.99	-3.29***
Freshman	-11118.55	-.20
Ideology (NJ composite)	3789.27	3.99***
Marginality	-1852.23	-.93
Seniority	-1110.45	-.27
State population (1000s)	17.35	4.88***
Temporal counter	87957.76	5.30***
Committee assignments		
Agriculture	-4017.26	-.08
Banking	-15690.48	-.33
Commerce	92437.20	2.00**
Energy	-48520.39	-1.08
Labor	-61917.59	-1.28
Small business	-45193.75	-1.01

Adjusted-R^2 = .59
N = 112

* p < .10, two-tailed test.
** p < .05, two-tailed test.
*** p < .01, two-tailed test.

receives approximately $180,000 more from corporate sources than does a Senator confronting an amateur opponent. Incumbents from large states similarly receive significantly more support from corporate PACs. No electoral marginality or seniority effects are evident. Strong relationships are not evident between most of the committee variables and capturing corporate support. Only Commerce Committee members receive substantially more support, approximately an additional $95,000, than all other Senators from corporate sources. Corporations are satisfied to support ideological friends and exploit vulnerable members, although the emphasis on Commerce Committee members suggests that corporate PACs attach some importance to areas of expertise and influence.

There is a substantial increase in corporate PAC allocations over time, even when controls for inflation are introduced, which may reflect a growing trend in business attempts to influence members of both parties. For example, the average Republican incumbent's con-

Table 3.3. *Labor PAC contributions*

Variable	Unstandardized coefficient	*t*-statistic
Constant	97072.31	
Challenger quality	5865.27	1.70*
Democrat	119257.70	5.95***
Freshman	4474.35	.20
Ideology (nj composite)	-1859.01	-4.87***
Marginality	1332.70	1.68*
Seniority	760.80	.46
State population (1000s)	.12	.08
Temporal counter	8881.59	1.34
Committee assignments		
Agriculture	-287.21	-.01
Banking	22348.72	1.18
Commerce	-7163.59	-.38
Energy	24911.81	1.37
Labor	7696.82	.39
Small business	10693.46	.59

Adjusted R^2 = .62
N = 112

* p < .10, two-tailed test.
** p < .05, two-tailed test.
*** p < .01, two-tailed test.

tributions from corporate interests increased from over $428,000 in 1982 to $705,000 in 1988. Campaign contributions to Democratic Senators also dramatically increased from an average of $162,000 in 1982 to over $433,000 in 1988. As a result, the ratio of average contributions obtained by Republicans compared to Democrats decreased from approximately 2.7:1 in 1982 to 1.6:1 by 1988.

Labor

Our data reveal that PACs linked to organized labor demonstrate a purely ideological contribution strategy. As the results in Table 3.3 indicate, committee assignments did not influence contributions from labor PACs. Instead, labor-based PACs offered the lion's share of their financial support to Democratic Senators in general and ideologically liberal Senators in particular. Democrats receive almost $120,000 more from labor PACs than Republicans.[7] As incumbents become more conservative, campaign contributions from labor quickly decrease. As a result, the most liberal Senators typically receive approximately $185,000 more than their more moderate counterparts.

Labor PACs also demonstrate definite responsiveness to potential incumbent vulnerability along several dimensions. Incumbents who face politically experienced opponents attract slightly more financial support than other incumbents. Marginal Senators similarly receive additional support from labor PACs, regardless of challenger profile. The difference in labor contributions received by an extremely marginal incumbent compared with an incumbent who was elected unopposed is almost $75,000. Seniority, state population, committee assignment, and temporal effects on labor giving are not evident. The growth in bipartisan giving evident among corporations during the 1980s was not observed among labor PACs. The average labor contribution to a Democratic Senator was 4.9 times greater than that garnered by a Republican in 1982. By 1988, average Democratic receipts were 20 percent greater than the amount captured in 1982, and the ratio of average Democratic receipts to Republican receipts had increased to 5.5:1.

Trade

Trade PACs demonstrated contribution strategies resembling those pursued by corporate PACs (see Table 3.4). Trade-association PACs responded to the same ideological cues as corporate PACs, although an explicit partisan effect is not evident. That is, conservative Senators receive substantially more support than liberal Senators from trade PACs, but Republicans received no explicit partisan advantage. For ultraconservatives, this translates into an additional $98,000 in campaign funds. Challenger quality also influences trade contributions. Incumbent Senators facing serious opposition typically attract greater financial support than Senators who face lower-quality candidates.

Substantial temporal effects are evident. All other variables held constant, a Senator running in 1988 received approximately $120,000 more from trade PACs than in 1982. From 1982 to 1988, the average campaign contribution to Democrats from trade PACs increased from $128,000 to $255,000. On the other hand, Republicans received even

Table 3.4. *Trade PAC contributions*

Variable	Unstandardized coefficient	t-statistic
Constant	110151.52	
Challenger quality	11537.39	2.90***
Democrat	-22043.32	-.95
Freshman	-24274.30	-.96
Ideology (NJ composite)	987.66	2.25**
Marginality	-245.62	-.27
Seniority	-2579.55	-1.37
State population (1000s)	2.18	1.33
Temporal counter	39386.26	5.13***
Committee assignments		
Agriculture	32437.96	1.44
Banking	7733.57	.35
Commerce	36195.47	1.70*
Energy	-28524.24	-1.37
Labor	-4540.81	-.20
Small business	5711.82	.27

Adjusted R^2 = .39

N = 112

* p < .10, two-tailed test.
** p < .05, two-tailed test.
*** p < .01, two-tailed test.

greater largesse. The average contribution for Republican incumbents increased from $230,000 to $342,000 over that time period. No seniority effects were apparent, and state size and marginality were insignificant. As was the case with corporate PAC contributions, the only committee whose members attracted more enhanced contributions was Commerce. Members of the Commerce Committee obtained an additional $36,000 more in campaign funds than other senators. Not surprisingly, for trade and corporate PACs, the members of this tax-writing committee are especially important regardless of the individual Senator's ideology or competition.

Cooperatives

The approximately sixty cooperative PACs are almost entirely aligned with farmers' cooperatives in the South and Midwest. Reflecting their highly specialized needs in terms of legislation, cam-

Table 3.5. *Cooperative PAC contributions*

Variable	Unstandardized coefficient	*t*-statistic
Constant	15686.75	
Challenger quality	576.07	.81
Democrat	244.46	.06
Freshman	-2768.09	-.61
Ideology (NJ composite)	-59.81	-.77
Marginality	14.72	.09
Seniority	-244.85	-.73
State population (1000s)	.11	.40
Temporal counter	701.10	.51
Committee assignments		
Agriculture	21964.86	5.53***
Banking	-3170.91	-.82
Commerce	2610.46	.69
Energy	-1733.45	-.47
Labor	-3193.66	-.80
Small business	1080.69	.29

Adjusted R^2 = .21
N = 112

* p < .10, two-tailed test.
** p < .05, two-tailed test.
*** p < .01, two-tailed test.

paign contributions from cooperative PACs are driven by a strategy that emphasizes accessing members of the Senate Agriculture Committee. Members of the committee receive approximately $22,000 more from cooperative PACs than other Senators. The presence of a highly focused contribution strategy, as revealed in Table 3.5, is not surprising. There are a relatively small number of cooperative PACs (approximately 60), and they are concerned with a highly focused area of economic regulation (agricultural subsidies).

Implications of targeted rent provision

The patterns of PAC allocations we observed indicate that Senators in the 1980s were well-positioned to exploit personal attributes such as ideology and party for financial support from major sources of PAC money, although the effects of committee assignment were more limited than observed in the House (see Grier and Munger, 1993, 1991).

Vulnerable incumbents are able to attract substantial support from particularized interests to fund reelection efforts. The three largest cohorts of PACs emphasize the incumbents who face tough challengers and the ideologically proximate incumbents. Significant temporal growth in trade and corporate contributions to incumbent Senators is evident during the 1980s, even with controls for inflation.

Senators also are able to selectively exploit their office and electoral position for substantial financial support from PACs. Trade, corporate, and labor PACs all respond to the past voting behavior of incumbents. Given their economic interests, it is not surprising that the direction and magnitude of giving reflects the traditional labor/business dichotomy (Eismeier and Pollock, 1986a). Corporate and trade-association PACs, however, demonstrate a more bipartisan campaign-contribution strategy toward Senators. By comparison, PACs linked to organized labor allocate most of their support for liberals and Democrats, who are obviously more likely to serve as advocates for labor interests.

The greater corporate support to Senators from larger constituencies and the general increase of trade and corporate support over time reveal that corporate and trade PACs continue to bankroll the reelection campaigns of incumbents, especially large-state campaigns. However, as the analyses in Chapter 2 indicate, increased reliance on PACs does not necessarily translate into greater efficiency in rent acquisition by incumbent Senators. Corporations and trade associations are directing revenues to incumbents who have high reelection costs due to their large constituency size and to members facing strong opponents. These same members are less likely to be able to retain funds after an election for war-chest building or quasi-legal expenditures (Parker, 1992a; Squire, 1991). This outcome suggests the costs of reelection are so high that maintaining a policy-entrepreneur position is of greater importance than campaign efficiency. This relationship also leaves incumbents vulnerable to the entreaties of rent-seeking interests who, if the vulnerable incumbents win reelection, will likely seek to collect on their investment.

The general lack of committee effects is consistent with prior studies by Grier and Munger (1993) and Grier, Munger, and Torrent (1990). In essence, legislative rules and institutional structures such as the filibuster allow all Senators to affect the flow of legislation (Sinclair, 1989). Therefore, special interests do not necessarily have to target their campaign funds on the basis of committee jurisdiction. Consequently, labor and business interests have greater freedom to reward friends and assist legislators who are seeking vulnerable campaign support. Special interests seeking potential access through campaign contributions need only locate sympathetic legislators who either want or need their financial support. The attractiveness for most organized interests of vulnerable or ideologically proximate incumbents is logical, given the desire to obtain particularized benefits.

The effect of the challenger-quality measure indicates that the targeting of Senators who need financial support for expensive or tough reelection fights is an inviting avenue for obtaining influence in the legislative process. Although we certainly are not arguing that marginal incumbents or incumbents who confront strong, experienced challengers seek those attributes in order to obtain contributions, those conditions may encourage such legislators to lower their "asking price" as a way to attract sufficient finances. Those financial allocations are likely to be dissipated in order to retain office, rather than being converted to personal use. However, as demonstrated in Chapter 2, the ability to retain large war chests is not positively related to PAC fund raising. Senators who are best able to retain their PAC contributions as rents are electorally secure discretion maximizers who have lowered constituency and reelection costs. In fact, incumbent Senators who rely most heavily on PAC funding for their reelections often have the least electoral flexibility and essentially are running simply to retain their seats.

4. Sitting in the cheap seats?

Campaigning is getting more expensive for everyone.

Richard F. Fenno
The United States Senate: A Bicameral Perspective

The previous two chapters have documented the conditions that affect rent acquisition and rent retention by U.S. Senators. The amount of money that changes hands in Senate campaigns is substantial and is driven by the electoral needs of incumbents. Interest groups often give based on partisan and ideological grounds. In this chapter, we assess the impact of spending on Senate elections.[1] Contrary to popular belief and unlike the phenomenal reelection rates enjoyed by House incumbents, tremendous turnover has occurred in the U.S. Senate. Table 4.1 reveals that from 1951 to 1993 the number of first-term Senators elected in a Senate class fell below 20 percent on only three occasions: 1961, 1983, and 1991, and went over 35 percent on ten occasions. In 1981, over half of incumbent Senators were serving their first term and 18 were newly elected. From 1981 through 1993, approximately one of every four Senators in each election class were freshmen. Between 1980 to 1992, 64 of the 231 elections held (27.7 percent) sent a new Senator to Capitol Hill. In fact, only 40 of the U.S. Senators holding office in 1993 served in the Senate before the administration of Ronald Reagan; and a number of incumbents opted not to seek reelection in 1994 for various reasons. The lower level of electoral security enjoyed by incumbents prior to 1988 contributes substantially to the motivation to build, and then use, war chests to maintain the policy-entrepreneur position.

Table 4.1. *Instances of freshman legislators, 1951-93*

Year	House		Senate		
	Freshmen	Freshman %	Newly elected	% in first term	
				In the class	In the chamber
1951	73	16.8	14 (14.4)[a]	38.8	54.0
1953	81	18.6	15 (15.4)	42.9	47.0
1955	56	12.9	14 (14.4)	36.8	43.0
1957	46	10.6	10 (10.4)	28.6	39.0
1959	79	18.2	16 (16.6)	47.1	40.0
1961	62	14.2	6	17.6	32.0
1963	67	15.2	10	25.6	31.0
1965	91	20.9	7	20.0	24.0
1967	73	16.8	7	20.0	24.0
1969	39	8.9	14	41.2	28.0
1971	56	12.9	11	31.4	32.0
1973	70	16.1	13	39.4	38.0
1975	92	21.1	11	32.4	35.0
1977	67	15.4	17	51.5	41.0
1979	77	17.7	20	57.1	48.0
1981	74	17.0	18	52.9	55.0
1983	81	18.6	5	15.1	43.0
1985	45	10.3	7	21.2	30.0
1987	50	11.5	13	38.2	25.0
1989	33	7.6	10	30.3	30.0
1991	44	10.1	4	11.4	27.0
1993	116	26.7	8	22.9	22.0

[a]Before 1960 the number of sitting U.S. Senators was 96. The number in parentheses is the percent freshmen legislators; after 1959, the number and percentage are identical.
Source: Data compiled by authors, and Stanley and Niemi (1991).

Senate elections in the United States

Assessing the impact of spending on congressional election outcomes has been one of the more intriguing problems addressed by
political scientists and economists. In the Senate, the problems of sufficient data points and inequities across constituencies have plagued
prior attempts to obtain meaningful results. Fortunately, examining
U.S. Senate elections from 1972 to 1990 allows us to test the linkage
between money and Senate election outcomes. We exclude uncon-
tested races as well as contested races where complete data are not
available from our analysis of the incumbent's share of the two-party
vote.[2] Of the 337 Senate elections held during this time period, 322

were contested and have complete data; 254 involved incumbent Senators.

Jacobson's work (1978, 1975) pioneered attempts to link campaign spending to outcomes in House elections. Subsequent research has explored campaign spending's impact on Senate election outcomes (Campbell and Sumners, 1990; Squire, 1991, 1989; Abramowitz, 1989, 1988). Typically, the party that is able to seize the spending advantage is assumed to benefit from the additional spending (Abramowitz and Segal, 1992; Campbell and Sumners, 1990). The mean spending advantage in Senate races from 1972 to 1990 was held by incumbents regardless of party.[3] The typical Democratic incumbent outspent the Republican challenger by $2.2 million to $1.3 million (constant 1990 dollars). Republican incumbents maintained a larger spending advantage, on average, than Democrats by outspending their challengers by $3.3 million to $1.8 million. Although the magnitude of spending advantage based on constant 1990 dollars is approximately equal for incumbents of both parties, the spending levels are much greater in terms of actual dollars for races involving Republican incumbents.[4] Republican incumbents held the spending advantage over their Democratic opponents in 85 percent of cases between 1972 and 1990. Democratic incumbents held the spending advantage over challengers in 86 percent of cases. This incumbency advantage was most pronounced in the late 1980s, when 93 percent of Democratic incumbents and 92 percent of Republican incumbents held the spending advantage over their opponents.

But, does a spending advantage translate into electoral advantage and eventual victory? Incumbent defeats may mean spending is less important than is generally thought in the political-science literature; or the marginal returns from spending may not be equal for incumbents and challengers. Measuring the effects of spending in Senate elections is more problematic than in House elections. The U.S. Senate is the only malapportioned legislative body in the United States. Costs of elections are not necessarily equal across all districts (states), indicating that candidates have variable electoral needs depending on the constituency in which they seek office. By comparison, in terms of population, House congressional districts are of approximately equal size or deviate only slightly in size from other districts. Measures of the impact of spending that assess the impact of total spending without regard for the basic electoral costs of running in the constituency will not reflect the actual influence of money in those elections. Ordinary least squares (OLS) regression equations of candidate total spending on Senate election outcomes reveal that challenger spending is significantly related to the incumbent vote share, whereas incumbent spending is nowhere near significance.

A second measure of spending proposed to control for population effects is the ratio of incumbent to challenger spending. For example, in a Democratic incumbent race, the amount of spending by the Democratic candidate minus the Republican candidate's spending is divided by total spending in the campaign by both candidates. The measure is bound from 1 (total Democratic advantage) to −1 (total GOP advantage), with 0 indicating equal spending. We contend that this measure, advanced by Campbell and Sumners (1990) is flawed. The spending ratio is predicated on the assumption that incumbents and challengers of both parties enjoy equal benefits from campaign spending, and ratio does produce a good fit with the vote for Senator ($R^2 = .61$). However, if spending does not decay at an equal rate for incumbents and challengers of both parties, then the decay rate of spending is not absorbed in the ratio, and the spending relationship is misspecified. Therefore, the ratio measure allows election outcomes to be explained but not predicted. Other research (see Grier, 1989) indicates that the returns from spending do diminish over time and that the marginal rates of return are not the same for incumbents and challengers (see also Silberman and Yochum, 1978).

The measure of spending we estimate is the spending per person in the state by each candidate. We maintain this is a superior measure for several reasons. First, all spending is standardized to control for potential inflationary effects. Second, spending is divided by population for Republican and Democratic candidates to obtain the dollars per person spent. As a result, the quadratic of the per-person spending allows us to estimate the differential rate at which the electoral returns of spending diminish based on party and incumbency status. Given the strong relationship between population and fund raising exhibited in the previous chapters, such an estimate of spending per person is likely to reflect the fund-raising calculus of legislators and challengers.[5]

In order to test the relationship between spending and vote outcome, we also include a series of independent variables as controls. The literature suggests candidate experience, national electoral trends, incumbency attributes, and temporal effects may exert effects on Senate election outcomes.

Candidate experience

Prior political experience is very important to election outcomes for the Senate. Squire (1989), for instance, finds a significant link between candidate political experience and the outcome of U.S. Senate elections. The most successful challengers to incumbent Senators typically are governors or House members. Prior research reveals candidate quality exerts a similar impact on House elections (Krasno and Green, 1988; Green and Krasno, 1988). Other political experience, such as a prior candidacy for a major office or a political appointment, or nonelective experience such as celebrity status may also enhance a candidate's electoral prospects (Squire, 1989; Krasno and Green, 1988).[6] Abramowitz and Segal (1992) note that the number of quality challengers is higher in Senate elections than in House elections. For example, from 1974 to 1986, thirty-six current or former House members sought a Senate seat occupied by an incumbent. Of those candidates, 44 percent were successful, indicating a rate of challenger success far greater than that of other challengers for other offices.

Using the Krasno and Green Index (see Chapter 3, note 4) allows us to capture a variety of candidate attributes, while also distinguishing between local elected officials such as mayors and city councilors and more prominent U.S. Representatives and statewide officials. The data presented in Table 4.2 illustrate the Democratic advantage in Senate challenger quality. When Senate elections are broken into three election cycles (1972, 1974, 1976; 1978, 1980, 1982; and 1984, 1986, 1988, 1990), the quality of Democratic candidates who challenge GOP incumbents declined after 1976, but increased in the latter part of the 1980s.[7] By comparison, Republican challengers ini-

Table 4.2. *Mean quality of challengers to incumbents, 1972-90*

	Challenger Party	
Cycle	Republican	Democrat
1972-76	3.36	4.60
1978-82	3.68	3.79
1984-90	3.48	3.82
1972-90	3.52	4.06

Source: Data compiled by authors. See discussion in Chapter 3, fn.4, for computation of the Krasno and Green Index of challenger quality.

tially increased in mean quality after the Watergate era, but then dropped slightly. In fact, Democrats consistently emerge as higher-quality challengers than Republicans. This probably is attributable to the higher level of lower-office political development of Democratic party candidate pools (Squire,1991, 1989; Ehrenhalt, 1991).

National electoral trends

National political factors may be related to Senate election outcomes. The higher profile exhibited by Senate campaigns implies that they may be more closely tied to national electoral swings (Abramowitz, 1980). Campbell and Sumners (1990) reinforce this contention by observing a relationship between presidential coattails and Senate elections since 1972. To test for the impact of national electoral effects, we measure coattails by the incumbent's party share of the presidential vote.[8] We also employ a dummy variable to indicate presidential election years. By doing so, midterm and presidential-election-year races can be pooled together. The dummy variable controls for the effects of the presidential election year, while preventing skewing of the coefficient by midterm elections, when coattails are by definition zero (Chubb, 1988).

Incumbency

Previous research indicates that incumbency, although not as overpowering as in House elections, is nonetheless important to the outcome of Senate elections (Campbell and Sumners, 1990; Jacobson, 1989; Kostroski, 1973).[9] Other studies have assumed all incumbents have identical response functions for campaign spending (Grier, 1989). In this study, we controlled for incumbency in the equation with dummy variables indicating the party of the incumbent (Campbell and Sumners, 1990). As noted above in the discussion of the specification of spending variables, we also examine challenger and incumbent spending without incorporating potential biases in the effects of spending through variable specification.

Temporal effects

In addition to these theoretically plausible variables, we use a temporal counter to control for changes in electoral strength over time (Campbell and Sumners, 1990; Bullock, 1988).

We estimate the following OLS equation:

$$Y = a + b_1X_1 + b_2X_2 + b_3X_3 + b_4X_4 + b_5X_5 + b_6X_6$$
$$+ b_7X_7 + b_8X_8 + b_9X_9 + b_{10}X_{10} + b_{11}X_{11}$$
$$+ b_{12}X_{12} + b_{13}X_{13} + e \qquad [6]$$

Where:

Y = Republican share of the two-party vote
X_1 = challenger political quality
X_2 = incumbent's party presidential vote
X_3 = presidential year dummy variable
X_4 = incumbency
X_5 = Democratic incumbent spending per voter
X_6 = quadratic of Democratic incumbent spending per voter (x_8^2)
X_7 = Republican incumbent spending per voter
X_8 = quadratic of Republican incumbent spending per voter (x_{10}^2)
X_9 = Democratic challenger spending per voter.
X_{10} = quadratic of Democratic challenger spending per voter (x_8^2).
X_{11} = Republican challenger spending per voter.

Table 4.3. *OLS regression estimates of Senate election outcomes*

Variable	Unstandardized coefficients	t-statistic
Constant	43.20	
Presidential election year	-5.27	-1.10
Presidential coattails	.16	1.93*
Incumbent party	-14.54	-11.66***
Challenger political quality	-1.15	5.11***
Republican incumbent spending	4.81	2.45**
Republican incumbent spending^2	-.36	-.89
Democratic incumbent spending	-10.99	-5.29***
Democratic incumbent spending^2	1.90	4.82***
Republican challenger spending	26.09	8.55***
Republican challenger spending^2	-6.80	-6.10***
Democratic challenger spending	-10.60	-6.00***
Democratic challenger spending^2	1.27	4.76***
Temporal control	.35	1.97**

Adjusted-R^2 = .73
N = 256

Numbers in parentheses are t-statistics. Dependent variable is the Republican two-party vote.
* p < .10, two-tailed test.
** p < .05, two-tailed test.
*** p < .01, two-tailed test.

X_{12} = quadratic of Republican challenger spending per voter (x_{10}^2)

X_{13} = temporal counter

e = error term.

Results

The regression analyses testing this proposition appear in Table 4.3.[10] The results of the analysis indicate that there is a strong, positive relationship between the per capita spending by incumbents and challengers of both parties. Coattail and challenger-quality effects are also evident. The adjusted-R^2 indicates that the equation explains almost three-quarters of the variance in incumbent Senate elections. Other studies, notably Abramowitz and Segal (1992) and Campbell and Sumners (1990), produce results that were no more robust. Neither of these studies specified the decay effect of spending in Senate elections, and they include a variety of constituency controls that do not alter the relationship between spending and election outcomes.[11]

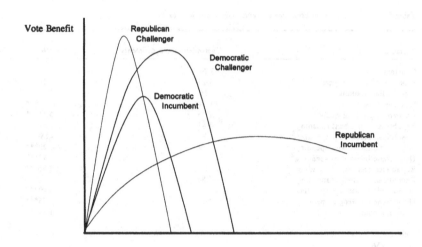

Figure 4.1. *Vote benefit from spending in Senate elections*

Because we are concerned with the effects and importance of *spending* in Senate elections, we opt for the more parsimonious, yet robust, equation presented here.

The use of quadratic terms to determine the point of diminishing returns from spending lends weight to our argument that the specification of comparative spending ratios is inappropriate to understanding the money–votes relationship. Figure 4.1 illustrates the dollars–votes relationship for the terms specified in Table 4.3. As indicated above, the marginal rate of return for spending is not equal for incumbents and challengers, or for candidates from the two major parties. Incumbents generally realize a smaller rate of return for their investment than challengers, who have a greater peak benefit from spending per voter. However, incumbents have a slower decay function for spending than challengers. Long after challengers reach the level of spending where they have diminished all positive returns, incumbents continue to derive benefits from increased spending.

Under the conditions demonstrated in Figure 4.1, it is intuitively obvious that incumbents should attempt to raise and spend far more money than their challengers. Because incumbents must spend substantially greater amounts of money than their opponents to attain a

Table 4.4. *Republican and Democratic electoral success and state population rank, 1972-90.*

Winning Party	State population rank			
	Top 10	Second 15	Third 15	Last 10
1972-76				
Republican	8	9	11	7
Democrat	10	23	19	13
1978-82				
Republican	7	17	18	12
Democrat	11	15	12	8
1984-90				
Republican	18	22	15	13
Democrat	15	25	20	7

Source: Data compiled by authors.

substantial vote benefit, early fund raising to build large war chests makes sense. For Republican incumbents from small western states, the ability to raise war chests far out of proportion to their populations is a politically beneficial strategy to pursue.

The small-state advantage

The relationship of per capita spending to Senate election outcomes underscores an advantage enjoyed by Republicans in Senatorial elections: the ability to exploit small-state Senate seats. The 25 smallest states contain only 16.2 percent of the nation's population, but elect half of the Senate's seats. Of those 50 seats, Republicans won only 18 of 50 (36 percent) from 1972 to 1976. After the Watergate era, however, Republicans exploited small-state opportunities by taking 30 of 50 seats (60 percent) from 1978 to 1982, and 37 of 70 (53 percent) from 1984 to 1990.

The disparity in Republican electoral success in large and small states becomes more apparent when we consider success by time period and state size. In Table 4.4, Senate election results for the early 1970s, late 1970s to early 1980s, and the late 1980s are arrayed by state size. In the early 1970s, Republican success was uniformly dismal although Republicans were most competitive in the ten largest

Table 4.5. *Spending per capita by incumbents and challengers, 1972-90*

| | Incumbents | | Challengers | |
State Rank[a]	Republican	Democrat	Republican	Democrat
Top 10	.77	.42	.22	.35
Second 10	.75	.39	.22	.40
Third 10	.84	.62	.37	.68
Fourth 10	1.41	.87	.63	.71
Bottom 10	2.41	2.09	1.26	1.21

[a] From largest to smallest.
Source: Data compiled by authors.

and ten smallest states. During the late 1970s and early 1980s, Republican success in Senate races was most pronounced in small states, where they won 60 percent of the elections, compared with about 40 percent of the large-state seats. By the late 1980s, Republicans still prevailed in the majority of small-state races. However, Democrats won almost two-thirds of Senate elections in states above the median population.

As we indicated in the analyses from Chapters 2 and 3, Senators from populous states raised more money from PACs, but were more likely to retain substantial war chests from their campaigns than Senators from smaller states. However, although large-market incumbents retain more money than other incumbents, they have to raise substantially larger amounts of money to attain reelection.[12] Therefore, from one electoral cycle to the next, Senators from small states should be able to retain more money, relative to their efforts, as a tangible asset. In addition, the fact that a Senator's influence is not contingent on state size makes small-state Senators a relative bargain for influence-seeking interests. For example, only one of eight Senators from the four largest states (California, New York, Texas, Florida) served before Reagan's presidency, and four are still serving their first term. By contrast, the Democratic and Republican floor leadership is from Maine, Kentucky, Kansas, and Wyoming, only one of which ranks above the national median for population (none are above the national mean). As a result, the data presented in Table 4.5 imply that Senators from smaller states can demand lower rents in the

Table 4.6. *Impact of mean campaign spending on Senate elections in small and large states*

| State rank[a] | Net vote benefit from spending | | | |
	Republican incumbents	Democrat incumbents	Republican challengers	Democra challeng
Top 10	2.42	3.77	5.09	3.38
Second 10	2.66	3.52	5.09	3.52
Third 10	2.64	5.35	8.21	6.32
Fourth 10	4.27	7.14	12.95	6.54
Bottom 10	6.89	13.01	20.81	10.42

[a] From largest to smallest.

Source: Computed from regression coefficients in Table 4.5

aggregate, but will be better positioned to retain long-term benefits. When one considers the mean expenditure per person by incumbents and challengers, controlling for state size and party, spending per capita is substantially greater in the smallest ten states. Relative expenditures decrease across incumbents and challengers as state size increases, until the top ten states are examined. Then, the average spending per capita increases slightly for Democratic and Republican incumbents. Challenger spending moves with state population, indicating that the advantage of small population is enjoyed by candidates from both parties. However, the fact that incumbents and challengers obtain marginal electoral benefits from campaign spending at differential rates works to the disadvantage of incumbents seeking reelection in less-populous states.

The mean rates of per capita spending in small-state races are much higher than for large states. For incumbents, it is imperative that they substantially outspend their challengers to negate the effects of challenger spending. If we calculate the swing in the two-party Senate vote based on the means for each of the five groups of states in Table 4.5, we find that incumbent Senators are more substantially disadvantaged in small states, due to the high level of per capita spending by incumbents and challengers (see Table 4.6). For a race in one of the ten largest states, when incumbent and challenger spending are set to mean values, Republican incumbents are disadvantaged by 0.96 percent against Democratic challengers, whereas Democratic incumbents lose 1.32 percent of the vote to Republican challengers. In the smallest ten states, the vote swing is more substantial. Republican incumbents lose a net 3.53 percent to Democratic challengers when spending per capita is held to the mean, whereas Democratic incumbents lose 6.20 percent net to Republican challengers. The relationships for the other cohorts of states indicate spending-to-votes impacts that fall roughly between these two extremes. Although Senators from less-populous states can seek reelection for a lower absolute cost than other solons, the ability of their challengers to field and bankroll competitive candidacies in smaller constituencies is a detriment to incumbent security. The turnover of multiple incumbents in the states of the northern-plain and southwestern states reflects the power of well-financed, experienced challengers in small states.

The relative cost per voter is much greater for individual incumbents in the smaller states than in large states. The higher levels of spending and the subsequent benefit challengers accrue indicates that even small-state incumbents need to spend substantial time and effort raising campaign funds for reelection fights. Although the amount of money necessary to finance an "extravagant" campaign in Maine, Nebraska or Montana would fund only a modest campaign in California or Texas, costs per voter are much higher for small-state incumbents. However, the commodity incumbents offer in the political market – influence in the policy-making process – is not institutionally diminished by the size of their physical constituency. Small-state incumbents can, therefore, finance campaigns that are extremely expensive *for their state*, but seek reelection for lower absolute costs compared to their colleagues.

As a result, with apologies to James Campbell (1993), small-state Senators sit in the real cheap seats. The costs of influencing a majority in the Senate are far less than in the House. This follows because to influence a majority in the U.S. House requires the provision of rents to individuals who have relatively fixed costs for reelection with regard to population. In the Senate, the costs to members to maintain entry barriers are more variable and require relatively small investments by interests in several legislators to forge a receptive caucus.[13] For a collection of interests seeking influence, targeting $100,000 to one large-state race may not be as prudent an investment as allocating $20,000 to incumbents in five races in less populous states, especially if those legislators have as much influence individually among their colleagues as the one legislator from the large constituency (Denzau and Munger, 1986). The relative benefit of the contribution to the Senator from a small state will be greater, given the proportional effect of money on per capita spending. For benefit-seeking interests, the provision of variable rents to Senate incumbents from smaller states is likely to decrease their aggregate investment without diluting access. Moreover, because the ability of individual Senators to affect the legislative process is greater than that of most House members, Senators from small states constitute potentially valuable investments for benefit-seeking interests seeking entree to the political arena.

5. Implications for campaign-finance reform

Abuses of campaign spending and private campaign financing do not stop at the other end of Pennsylvania Avenue. They dominate congressional elections as well.

Senator Edward M. Kennedy
Congressional Quarterly Weekly Report, October *11, 1974*

In the preceding chapters, we have presented an argument in support of the notion that U.S. Senators' behavior resembles that of rent-seeking firms in a competitive market. This chapter presents the findings from those chapters in a comprehensive fashion so we can assess alternatives to the present system of campaign finance. We discuss the impact of various campaign-finance reform proposals on candidate rent acquisition and, therefore, Senate election outcomes. Specifically, we examine lower political-action-committee (PAC) contribution limits, PAC abolition, public financing, matching funds, and spending caps. Ultimately, each reform results in a paradox that is not necessarily an improvement over the preexisting rent-seeking system. For example, spending caps confront constitutional problems, some of which are set forth in *Buckley v. Valeo* [424 U.S. 51 (1976)]. Even if constitutionally permissible, others have referred to caps as incumbent protection, making the task of defeating an incumbent almost impossible (see Thomas, 1989; Silberman and Yochum, 1978; Jacobson, 1976). Public financing may not be feasible given existing federal deficits. Matching funds transfer capital outlays for campaigns to the government, but still require candidates to raise money, leaving open the potential for rent seeking. The newest potential reform, term limits, appears to present a nonfinancial solution to the entrenched incumbent. Although term limits produce turnover, they do not preclude rent seeking while in office and, therefore, constitute an inferior solution to the problems associated with incumbent government.

Evidence of rent seeking in Senate elections

The results of our analysis indicate that Senators' behavior does reflect the behavior of rent-seeking firms in a constrained market. Legislators continue to devote more time and energy to raising financial support for their campaigns. Special interests, which typically seek rents from government, are placed in the position of providing substantial rents to legislators in exchange for policy. Economic interests demonstrated remarkably sophisticated strategies for allocating their largesse. The need of legislators to obtain these subsidies in order to gain reelection has resulted in an institution whose members are engaged in a predominantly inefficient venture. Most rents are either dissipated in retaining the policy-entrepreneur position, or the effort at retaining the market position is unsuccessful, thereby ending the entrepreneur's career in the policy market.

Time is money

Senators substantially increased their off-year fund raising during the 1980s. Controlling for inflation, the amount of early money raised by Senators doubled during the 1980s. By 1988, the average amount of preemptive money raised by a Senator *not up for reelection in the current cycle* was greater than the average amount of money raised by House incumbents seeking reelection.

Raising early money was primarily an activity of legislators who, for a variety of reasons, could be considered electorally vulnerable. Senators who diminished their war chests during their prior election campaign were prone to raise substantially greater early money from PACs. Immediately upon arriving in the Senate, freshman legislators raised more money than other Senators, especially from PACs. Large opposition candidate pools also drove fund raising across all time periods, although it had no effect on PAC receipts.

Men of the House

One of the more interesting relationships uncovered was the ability of prior House membership on fund raising and campaign efficiency.

Former House members displayed no greater proclivity for raising money in early or middle cycles of their term than any of their fellow Senators. Former Representatives in the Senate were much more adept at raising PAC money during the reelection cycle. Compared to other Senators, former House members retained substantially larger campaign surpluses after reelection. Over 60 percent of former House members in the Senate were initially elected to Congress in, or after, 1974. Many of these members moved to the Senate after 1978. The changes observed in Senate fund-raising behavior coincide with the movement of modern politicians into the Senate. This coincidence may explain the growth of electoral and fund-raising behavior previously confined to the House.

Hitting running targets

The PAC allocation patterns to Senators reinforces the rent-seeking behavior evident in Chapter 2. If PACs did not contribute to candidates in order to further their own political and economic interests, a random contribution pattern would be observed. If strategies only reflected the desire of PACs to support friends, no significant indicators beyond measures of ideological proximity or party would be evident. Neither of these conditions exclusively prevail in the PAC analysis. Instead, effects beyond ideological and partisan influences are evident in allocations by labor, corporate, trade, and cooperative PACs. There are strong influences by indicators of candidate vulnerability, constituency size, and occasional institutional influences (committee assignments). The extremely precise nature of PAC cohort allocations reflects a pragmatic strategy of giving not only to friends, but also of lending assistance to legislators who need electoral support. Our own research on the allocation patterns of polluting industries indicate that these relationships are more precise within specific areas of regulation (Regens, Gaddie, and Elliott, 1994, 1993; Regens, Elliott, and Gaddie, 1991).

The existence of sophisticated PAC allocation strategies reinforces the notion that Senators can act as policy entrepreneurs. If policy allocations did not influence PAC giving, random allocation decisions would be evident. The allocations of PACs, however, reflect the Denzau and Munger policy-pricing model. Political action committees allocate money to receptive legislators who will support – or have provided – favorable policy. Allocations are also made to legislators who have lower purchase prices, due to the need to externalize campaign costs or in order to counter perceived vulnerabilities.

Campaign costs

The need for legislators to seek external financial help is an outgrowth of the prominent role of money in Senate elections. In Chapter 4, we noted that incumbents generally maintained the spending advantage over challengers and that maintaining the advantage was extremely important to electoral success. Challengers derive greater initial benefits from per capita spending than do incumbents, although those benefits decay rapidly as spending increases. Incumbents enjoy a slower decay rate of electoral return for spending. Because high-quality challengers present formidable electoral obstacles to incumbents, efforts to deter potential challengers make intuitive sense.

The per capita spending relationship has interesting implications for the allocation of rents in Senate elections. The fact that Senators have highly variable reelection costs indicates that members will not have to make equal investments in fund raising. For incumbents from smaller states, the fact that their per vote cost of reelection is relatively high is offset by the substantially lower reelection costs when compared to their colleagues. Because the influence of members in the chamber is independent of population effects, policy-seeking interests can potentially purchase more influence for less cost if they shop Senators from small states. The relatively lower costs of reelection allow those legislators to more selectively seek and obtain rents from interest groups, thereby preserving their discretion.

PAC strategy

Our analysis reinforces the notion of selective contribution strategies by PACs. The trends observed are indicative of a strategy that is becoming increasingly prevalent even among major PACs known for giving widely and often to candidates. The National Realtors' PAC has announced its intention to cut contributions from $4 million in 1992 to a little less than $2.5 million for the 1994 elections. The committee intends to abandon its self-described "carpet-bombing" strategy of giving money to virtually every congressional and senatorial campaign. Instead, the Realtors–PAC will allocate funds to races where their money will do the most good and have the greatest impact. If legislators have to compete for a smaller pool of rents, the competition should be more intense. If that is the case, the provision price for policy will be lowered further as legislators attempt to capture part of a limited amount of rents. An increasingly particularized PAC contribution strategy should then result in even more rent seeking and competitive policy provision by legislators.

Reforming elections and campaign finance

Increasing public awareness of the financial disparities between legislators and their opponents, and the degree to which these disparities are reflected in election outcomes, propelled substantial campaign-finance reform proposals onto the political agenda in the 1990s (see Alston, 1991a, 1991b). Proposed campaign-finance reforms include, but are not limited to, removing party contribution limits, eliminating PACs, imposing aggregate candidate-spending limits, public financing of elections, matching funding of elections, and various combinations of these reforms. Each reform will affect the flow of money entering political campaigns, but these reforms also have potential drawbacks that may result in outcomes not intended by reformers. Some fail to adequately reconcile the disparity between incumbent and challenger financial support; others are politically difficult to enact. Many of them could have an impact similar to the 1974 Federal Election Campaign Act (FECA), further entrenching incumbents. If this is the case, reform of the congressional campaign system will prove to be exactly what the advocates of reform *did not* have in mind.

Free the parties

One proposed change in the congressional campaign-finance laws is to free the parties from existing spending and contribution limits.

This option is attractive to Republicans because it theoretically allows them to bury Democrats under an avalanche of party money. The long-held Republican advantage in national-party fund raising presumably would enable Republicans to direct substantially more money into competitive candidacies. The removal of party spending limits imposed under the Federal Elections Commission (FEC) would allow the GOP to overwhelm their less well financed Democratic opponents. Just as reality does not usually conform to fairy tales, removing the restraints of campaign finance will not work exclusively to the advantage of the GOP. Ending limits on use of party money will not necessarily result in tremendous influxes of money to Republican candidates.[1] Instead, parties may find themselves increasingly pressed by incumbents and challengers for money, while these same legislators continue to seek rents elsewhere.

If parties selectively allocate financial support to candidates when the per-candidate allocation is limited but the candidate population is effectively inexhaustible, there is no rationale to believe that candidates who were not funded under the former system would receive support if the limit on funding were lifted. Instead, the candidates to whom parties maximized support would be likely to gain even more money. Because many interest groups will continue to pursue their highly particularized goals, parties may not be able to attract sufficient funds to channel to incumbents. Political action committees and individuals could still go directly to legislators for selective benefits. For incumbents, continuing the PAC system will be beneficial, if only because they will be positioned to provide selective benefits to – and extract financial support from – interest groups, while also capturing even more money from the newly freed party coffers.

PAC reform

Another proposed change in the campaign-finance system is to restrict or eliminate PACs (Alston, 1991a). Political action committees originally were approved as part of campaign-finance reform in the early 1970s. By bringing campaign finance into the sunshine, the 1974 FECA was intended to avert future abuses of campaign money (Sabato, 1985). As a result, although most of the accounting of political contributions takes place in the open, these PACs have nonetheless become a vehicle for political influence of incumbent legislators (Munger, 1989; Wright, 1989; Poole and Romer, 1985; Sabato, 1985). Moreover, as spending gaps between challengers and incumbents become more pronounced, the cries to reform PACs have become more pronounced.

Three avenues of PAC reform exist. First, some reformers advocate placing more stringent limits on the size of PAC contribution. The second proposed reform involves limiting the amount of money a candidate can receive from PACs, by capping total PAC contributions with either a flat cap or by a percent-of-funding formula. The most radical break with the current system would be the abolition of PACs (Alston, 1991a). Although each of these options hinders efforts to channel money to incumbents, there is no guarantee that PAC reform will narrow the spending gap between incumbents and challengers. Changes in the rules of the game can be subverted with creativity on the part of contributors and candidates.

Reducing the size of PAC contributions obviously will decrease the amount of PAC money that candidates can receive from individual committees. The problem arising from such limitations is that the limits will not necessarily serve to reduce the total contributions from PACs to candidates. Political action committees do not necessarily give the maximum allowable contribution to candidates, but often make symbolic contributions. With over four thousand PACs in the United States, the potential amount of PAC money a candidate can receive is staggering, even if the maximum PAC contribution is limited to $500 or even $100. Reducing the maximum individual PAC contribution does not necessarily reduce the total receipts by incumbents from cartels of PACs that informally follow coordinated contribution strategies. In Chapter 2, we also note that the majority of Senate candidates raised more money from individuals than PAC sources. This indicates that incumbent fund-raising advantages are not limited to PACs.

Capping the potential aggregated receipts incumbents obtain from PACs could have an opposite effect to that desired by reformers. Election costs are largely related to population size and media costs. Fund raising by incumbents from PACs similarly reflects population effects. If PAC fund raising is capped with a flat cap, incumbents from small states will be positioned to raise substantial amounts of their war chests from interest groups. By comparison, large-state incumbents will need to place additional emphasis on raising funds from individuals and will also push harder for party support. Senators from less populous states, by contrast, may be more susceptible to interest-group entreaties. Therefore, they may be more prone to seeking rents for themselves.

Another alternative would cap the amount of money candidates receive from all PAC sources at 20 percent of all receipts (Boren-Byrd-Ford bill). Political action committees would continue to be able to give a total of $5,000 to an individual candidate per election. Under such a campaign-finance regime, legislators could find themselves increasingly dependent on a few PACs for funding, if only because these committees could more selectively shop the electoral market with the knowledge that the maximum asking price from an incumbent has been capped. Political action committees may be able to further ingratiate themselves to incumbents by denying challengers any substantial funding.

Abolishing PACs will curtail the incumbent funding advantage more than simply constraining PAC contributions. Political action committees are the second largest source of Senate candidate financial support, after contributions from individuals (Stanley and Niemi, 1992; Jacobson, 1989). PAC support is disproportionately lavished on incumbents, indicating that incumbents will bear the brunt of abolishing this source of money (Sabato, 1985). Conversely, because PACs are typically affiliated with interest groups or corporations that exist beyond the structure of the PAC, and derive large amounts of money from individuals (Sabato, 1985), special interests may go "off book" and attempt to coordinate the contribution patterns of individuals to candidates through informal organizations. For example, firms may informally encourage executives to support certain candidates through direct contributions.

Political-action-committee reform should make incumbent fundraising efforts more difficult. However, the nature of proposed PAC reforms do little to necessarily elevate the financial profiles of challengers. Abolishing PACs might return some political power to the parties, although existing limits on party support would need to be lifted in conjunction with meaningful PAC reform.

Candidate spending limits

Spending limits have been part of proposals to reform campaign finance for over two decades and were incorporated into the 1974 FECA. Under the 1974 FECA proposal, the limits to candidate spending were uniform across congressional districts and varied based on population in Senate races. More recent proposals for voluntary limits pegged to the receipt of public financing or matching funds echo earlier post-Watergate reforms, by establishing a population-based formula to set Senate limits. The perceived impact of such limits remains controversial, and regulation that some perceive as reform is considered an "incumbency protection act" by others (Jacobson, 1976). If there is no deleterious impact of spending limits on challenger performance, then the imposition of such limits on spending in prior elections should not alter their outcomes. Abramowitz (1989), for instance, found little evidence that a meaningful impact by proposed spending limits was evident when simulating the 1986 races.

The Silberman–Yochum model of campaign spending provides one of the earliest conceptualizations of the impact of campaign spending on candidate vote support (see also Jacobson, 1978, 1976; Glantz, Abramowitz, and Burkart, 1976). It posits that, although candidate spending affects candidate performance, attempts to limit campaign expenditures would not lead to a further "incumbency advantage" by precluding strong challengers from spending enough money to defeat incumbents. In operationalizing challenger and incumbent spending for the 1972 and 1974 elections, Silberman and Yochum (1978) differentiate between the effects of spending by party and include a quadratic of spending to test for diminishing returns from increased spending. Spending is significant for incumbents and challengers of both parties. The model is then reestimated with the addition of interaction terms between length of incumbency (short- versus long-term), challenger status, and expenditures. The model is also estimated separately for each party. These estimates are then used to differentiate between the size and rate of diminishing returns from spending for each type of candidate. Positive returns from spending diminish quickly for short-term (first- or second-term) incumbents, more slowly for long-term incumbents, and most slowly

for challengers. Silberman and Yochum find that all candidates, challenger and incumbent alike, reach the point of diminished returns
from campaign spending before the $188,000 spending limit. Limits
on spending, therefore, may not be as desultory as Common Cause
maintains (see also Jacobson, 1976).

But is the Silberman–Yochum hypothesis accurate? The underlying assumption that spending limits do not serve to protect incumbents because the marginal returns from spending are diminished
before the cap is reached is erroneous. Spending caps are set by legislators, who have a vague knowledge of the returns they obtain from
spending. The fact that one limit does not create an incumbency advantage does preclude setting the limit to the point where potential
challenger benefits are foregone due to those limits. If campaign-
finance limits were set lower, the outcome of reform could be highly
beneficial to incumbents. In the Silberman–Yochum model, when
campaign spending is limited to the point at which an incumbent's return for an additional dollar spent is zero but challengers still accrued
a positive benefit from additional spending, incumbents would benefit from spending limits. As Figure 5.1 shows, setting the limit on expenditures at the point where long-term incumbents cease to accrue
benefits from spending preempts a small benefit to short-term incumbents (triangle ABC) from spending. Challengers, however, are
preempted from realizing a rather sizable benefit over long-term incumbents (triangle BDE) as well as a benefit over short-term incumbents (trapezoid ACDE). In this case, the campaign expenditure limit
prevents challengers, however unlikely their ability to raise funds,
from exploiting their potential financial resources against incumbents.

The marginal benefit curves presented in Figure 5.1 are incorrect.
Despite using a quadratic decay, Silberman and Yochum's marginal
return curves present a linear, rather than a curvilinear, rate of return.
The estimates of Senate election returns in Table 4.3 indicate that the
returns from spending initially climb, then peak, and finally diminish, as illustrated in Figure 4.1. The marginal returns for incumbents
are less than for challengers; however, challengers reach the point of
diminished returns from spending before incumbents.

Consider also that incumbents will set the campaign-spending limits. If incumbents have some notion of when their marginal benefits

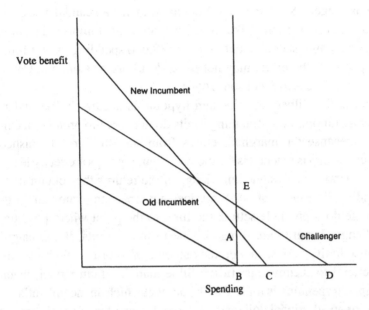

Figure 5.1. *The model of campaign-spending returns presented by Silberman and Yochum*

from spending are exhausted, it is logical to assume they will set spending limits at some point where incumbents have obtained all their marginal benefits, but where limits prevent challengers from deriving additional benefits from outspending incumbents. If spending caps are set where challenger marginal benefits have just become exhausted but incumbent marginal benefits were previously exhausted, challengers continue to reap considerable benefits from spending that incumbents cannot offset. Incumbents, therefore, should attempt to set spending limits at some level at, or near, their own diminished returns. By setting a limit at, or before, the level at which they diminish their benefits, incumbents do not derive any direct benefit; however, they do preempt potential challenger benefits from increased spending.

Public financing

Public financing is often mentioned in conjunction with spending limits. Critics of spending caps recognize that incumbents will be ad-

vantaged under spending caps because challengers will still face dif-
ficulties raising money. One solution is to create a system of public finance and matching funds. Recent proposals provide dollar-for-dollar
matching funds including funds to compensate for opponent spending-
cap violations and excessive independent expenditures on behalf of
opponents (see Alston, 1991a, 1991b). These proposals, incorporated
into the legislation vetoed by President Bush in early 1992, would
have upped the level of challenger fund raising to levels on a par with
incumbents and introduced a mechanism for punishing defectors who
violated the imposed limits.[2] Despite the fact that mathematic models
indicate no enhanced electoral benefit for challengers when spending
caps and matching-funds systems are imposed (Thomas, 1989), fundamental differences between the Republican and Democratic parties
concerning the role of the government in subsidizing elections has led
to Republican opposition of public financing as a reform.

Any reform of the campaign-finance system will be sensitive to the
political desires of those individuals making the changes as well as
the anticipated reaction of voters (Denzau and Munger, 1986). It certainly is possible that reform could enhance challenger profiles. But,
the enactment of reform that bolsters the financial quality of candidates may face public resistance. Given the hostility of many voters
to congressional pay raises and honoraria, the reaction to subsidizing
a billion dollar campaign and advertising industry is likely to be even
more negative.

The impact of reform on rent seeking

The success of incumbents in retaining office year after year has
prompted calls to reform the political system. The underlying assumption is that something is "wrong" with the Congress and that the
members of Congress are the source of the problem. Yet most proposed reforms of the electoral system do not disrupt the rent-seeking
relationship between legislators and interest groups. For example, because interest groups are still able to access and influence candidates,
the linkage between candidates and interests is not likely to be ended
by term limits. Resources simply will shift from one legislator to the
next as turnover displaces old incumbents. Spending limits also are

not likely to eliminate rent seeking and rent provision. If spending limits are not accompanied by fund-raising limits, there is no rationale for assuming that incumbents will not continue to build war chests beyond their existing financial needs. Even if fund-raising limits are imposed, spending limits not accompanied by some form of public financing or matching funds will leave challengers underfunded. Conventional election research indicates that the problem of money in politics is not too much money, but rather too little, especially for challengers. The disparity between incumbents and challengers frequently leads to the perception of money being at the root of "bad" politics. As a result, if the problem is one of funding challengers, the campaign-finance system must be constructed to make challengers more attractive investments.

6. Reform and the rent-seeking legislature

Each, in consequence, has a greater regard for his own safety or happiness, than for the safety or happiness of others; and, where these come in opposition, is ready to sacrifice the interests of others to his own.

John C. Calhoun
Disquisition on Government

Personal abuse, constant tension, limited financial return, disorganized and dislocated personal life, and a multitude of uncertainties all serve to discourage good men from service in Congress.

Former Congressman Frank E. Smith
Congressman From Mississippi

Economists have long held that potentially contestable assets will attract investment in direct proportion to their production capabilities. A standard assumption in the public choice literature is that the relationship between politicians and economic interests can be modeled in a manner similar to market exchanges. Presumably, politicians are in a position to extract rents from interested parties by providing selected benefits such as regulatory policies favorable to industry or other stakeholders in the political process. Our analysis demonstrates how the concept of rent seeking enhances understanding of political-action-committee (PAC) strategies, since PACs possess the capability of allocating financial resources to candidates as differential rents. Among legislators, the ability to produce policy outputs for particularized interests can be viewed as an exercise that allows members to place an implicit price on outputs. Benefit-seeking interests can bid for outputs in an effort to gain additional remuneration in the market through government subsidy or other implicit wealth transfer, such as monopoly regulation. Such benefits, which exist beyond the marginal costs of production in a competitive market, are considered rents; and the firms who pursue them, rent seekers (Tullock, 1980b, 1965).

Under the existing campaign-finance regime, a political market has evolved that allows legislators to extract financial support for electoral campaigns. There is overwhelming evidence that the contribution strategies of special interests coincide with their rational self-interest. In turn, legislators are able to exploit their office for financial return or extra pay (Parker, 1992a). Legislators with relatively low marginal costs for retaining office will be able to extract higher rents than other legislators. For example, although the gross rents obtained by Senators from large states may be greater than those rents obtained by Senators from small states, this relationship does not necessarily translate into greater efficiency in retaining rents, especially when legislators increasingly rely on PAC support for their rents, or dissipate their rents to retain office. Thus, by using the theoretic framework of rent seeking to examine legislator behavior, we are able to move beyond the traditional correlates of the campaign-contribution approach to a more substantive understanding of how special-interest money and lawmakers are linked. Conceptualizing legislators as firms in a limited oligopoly market allows us to understand the motivation behind the maintenance of the existing campaign-finance system and explains how such a system helps construct legislator behavior. This framework allows us to assess PAC and legislator behavior using a theoretic rationale that is both intuitively pleasing as well as intellectually appropriate given the behavior demonstrated by legislators.

Rent seeking in the campaign-finance system

Although the campaign-finance system acts as a form of protective regulation that allows incumbents to extract extra compensation, or rents, from benefit-seeking interests, the degree to which legislators profit from rent-seeking behavior is unclear. Occasionally legislators who are reelected have dissipated all of their rents and must therefore continue substantial rent-seeking behavior into the next term of office.[1] The increase in early fund raising, particularly by junior and vulnerable Senators, indicates that such a phenomenon is evident. This relationship contributes substantially to the proliferation of rent-seeking activity through campaign fund raising.

However, Senators who are able to run superefficient reelection campaigns are less likely to have diminished war chests and will therefore need to concentrate less on preemptive fund raising than do other members. By freeing themselves from the cycle of constant fund raising, these members have greater discretion in their ability to allocate time toward legislation and policy concerns of importance to themselves (Parker, 1992b). With greater discretion comes the ability to selectively choose interests to support or to provide policy outputs. The decline of the marginal cost of policy creation these members enjoy enables them to extract contributions as rents and disperse those rents with greater discretion than a legislator who is offsetting existing campaign debt or attempting to preempt potential challengers. In fact, the most successful rent seekers are not those members who obtain the most PAC contributions. Instead, the members who retain contributions, preempt strong challengers, and maximize their discretion in the chamber *and* in the constituency are the most efficient.

Reforms that seek to curtail or eliminate the rent-seeking relationship between legislators and special interests will necessarily require the elimination of PACs. However, this alone is unlikely to eradicate rent seeking by legislators in the campaign-finance system. In fact, reforms that constrain PAC support will only reconstruct the calculus by which rent seeking occurs.

Does the present system work?

The U.S. Senate is an electorally responsive institution. Turnover of U.S. Senators through defeat and retirement is more dramatic than in the House. The Senate changed majority party twice in a six-year period during the 1980s, and neither party has held a secure majority since 1977. Senators face strong challengers who are politically experienced (Squire, 1991, 1989). Challengers for Senate seats are electorally competitive and are able to obtain substantial benefits from spending. Incumbents are pressed to raise funds and defend highly visible positions on various policy matters (Sinclair, 1989).

It is precisely this responsiveness that makes rent-seeking behavior not only acceptable but necessary from the vantage point of many

Senate members. Senators increasingly come to the Senate from the post-Watergate House of Representatives. This generation of legislators pioneered, perfected, and then exploited the modern campaigning techniques that define contemporary politics. These techniques, which emphasize constituency contacting, continuous campaigning, and substantial fund raising, led many House members to emphasize constant fund raising in order to deter challengers and build electoral security. As these members moved into the Senate, they brought many of these year-round fund-raising and electioneering habits to the chamber. Other members, who had not necessarily served in the House, nonetheless pursued similar strategies and used these techniques in gaining a Senate seat. Individuals such as Alphonse D'Amato or Donald Riegle exemplify the extreme transition of the Senator from deliberator to constituency ombudsman, policy entrepreneur, and fund raiser.[2]

Rent seeking in decline?

In her seminal study of the U.S. Senate, Barbara Sinclair (1989) indicates that the institutional structures of the U.S. Senate reflect the needs of the legislator. The decline of seniority and specialization norms, the acceptance of the show horse, and the decline of institutional loyalty all reflect the needs of modern politicians in their pursuit of political influence and reelection. Changes in the campaign-finance system reflect similar needs on the part of legislators. The strong linkage between the ideology and the vulnerability of U.S. Senators and the sources from which they derive campaign-finance support indicate that the campaign-finance regime is part of the institutional structure of the Senate. If the existing system is no longer profitable, due either to the demands on time and autonomy in the chamber or external costs arising from constituency disaffection, then Senators will embrace reform.

With the spurt of recent Senate retirements, many legislators have noted the tremendous costs of fund raising as one reason for leaving the Senate. Senator Dennis Deconcini, a long-time advocate of campaign-finance reform, indicated that he was "sick of the fund raising. We need substantive campaign-finance reform." Taken as just one example, Deconcini's statement reflects the growing reality of the existing campaign-finance system.[3] Demands for money to seek reelection are so great that the levels of contributions are not sufficient to simultaneously retain reelection, satisfy constituency needs (Denzau and Munger, 1986), pursue legislation or policy imperatives with autonomy, and still retain the desire to continue in the Senate.

Given such an environment, Senators will seek to reform the campaign-finance system in order to free their policy autonomy and at least maintain or increase their electoral security. As we demonstrated in Chapter 4, incumbent Senators are more vulnerable and the Senate is subject to greater turnover than the U.S. House of Representatives (see Abramowitz, 1980). As a result, future changes in the campaign-finance system will be designed to give incumbent Senators the electoral security that has been prevalent in House elections.

The problem of campaign reform and self-regulation

Rent-seeking behavior among Senators is a historic reality, exemplified in the 1890 Thomas Nast cartoon of the giant "Trusts," depicted as great money bags, sitting in the gallery of the Senate. The exploitation of public office for private gain did not originate with the PAC system and it will not be eradicated by its abolition. What the creation of PACs permitted researchers to do is to trace and model the relationships between economic interests and legislators in a systematic fashion, thereby allowing us to readily identify the monetary dimension of special-interest influence. As a result, before changing the campaign-finance system, the question of how reform will affect the legislature must be considered. Because Senators will perceive a visible time horizon for their legislative career, even if campaign finance is eliminated as a mechanism for the provision of variable benefits, they may use their policy position to ensure future employment or a postlegislative career (Lott, 1990). Rents need not be collected until well into the future, especially if the deferred benefits are substantial.

Public financing has been advanced as a potential avenue for the elimination of the unsavory aspects of campaign finance, which we assume includes the provision of particularized benefits to special interests and legislators. By providing public funding, an assumption is made that legislators will be able to pursue the creation of broad public goods, free from the pressures of benefit-seeking interests or the need to raise and maintain war chests. However, even the provision of public financing does not guarantee that rent seeking will be removed from the Senate. Because a Senate seat is a monopoly position that is contestable, potential legislators will bid up its price in an effort to obtain the policy position, and candidates will attempt to externalize the financial effort of seeking office (see Paul and Wilhite, 1990). By doing so, the costs of rent seeking are not born by the office seeker. As a result, public financing effectively externalizes all but the opportunity cost of seeking office. Any attempt at reforming Congress and the behavior of its members will have to pass through both legislative chambers. If legislators are rational, rent-seeking individuals, as we contend, then although reforms originating with Congress will necessarily be responsive to public opinion, they will not necessarily disadvantage incumbent legislators. We maintain that the existing campaign-finance system, which was lauded at the time of its inception as a step toward reform of money in politics, illustrates this point. Subsequent experience has shown that special interests and legislators have been able to use the current system as a vehicle for the indirect compensation of legislators. The behavior of PACs reveals precise, sophisticated strategies for targeting legislators whose support reflects the policy priorities of those PACs. Coincidentally, the institution evolved to the advantage of the individual members, and the systematic production of policy suffered. The resultant behavior of Senators in the wake of the post-Watergate campaign-finance reforms indicates that similar effects were felt in the system of campaign finance.

Postmortem

The recent fight over campaign-finance reform in the Congress reflects the problem of security and satisfaction with the current system, the exercise of discretion by legislators, and the effect of self-regulation. The 1992 campaign-finance bill, which passed both the House and the Senate, included provisions for voluntary spending caps, matching funds to offset independent expenditures, and limits on the ability to accept PAC money. Senate elections had spending and fund-raising caps pegged to population, and House campaigns had universal spending and fund-raising caps. The legislation cleared both chambers and was vetoed by President Bush. There was insufficient support in both chambers to override the president's veto.

In 1993, President Clinton indicated that he would sign a campaign-finance-reform law similar to the one passed by Congress and vetoed in 1992. Despite the infusion of self-styled, reform-minded legislators into both chambers, the coalition that passed the campaign-finance legislation in 1992 was unable to reconstitute in both chambers. The Senate passed legislation similar to that vetoed by President Bush in 1992. The House passed campaign-finance legislation that contained few changes from the existing campaign-finance system. In fact, as a self-regulating enterprise, Congress evidences little likelihood of imposing effective limits. Fred Wertheimer, president of Common Cause, underscores this reality by noting: "If we're going to reform this system, we have to put an end to members of Congress living off their campaign money. What you end up with here is special-interest groups not only financing the campaigns of Congress, but their personal lifestyles as well" (Wartzman, 1994:A12). Our own analysis provides ample support for concluding that, in practice, incumbent lawmakers will pursue a wide latitude in seeking and retaining campaign funds for discretionary use.

Notes

Introduction

1. The use of the concept of an economic rent is substantially different from its conventional connotation in which a rent is the price paid by one party to use an object, such as a dwelling or car, owned by another party to the transaction.
2. For example, government regulation during the Nixon administration provided milk producers a substantial subsidy after they made large contributions to the Nixon reelection effort.
3. The area bounded by triangle CEF represents the dead-weight loss to society from rent seeking.
4. We recognize that PACs give financial contributions to candidates for a variety of reasons. Some provide unsolicited contributions in order to reward or win friends. Other PACs give because they are solicited by incumbents and are afraid to refuse.

1. The Senate in transition and campaign finance

1. A hold is a grant of twenty-four hours' notice by the leadership of an issue coming to the floor. Members who invoked holds did so to signal to the leadership that they have problems with the legislation, and that an opportunity to negotiate existed. According to interviews by Sinclair (1989) with legislative staffers, holds have become effective vetoes, with members using holds to "strike" legislation they oppose strongly.
2. Interestingly enough, despite the reforms of the 1970s, this remains a practice still found under the campaign-finance regime established by FECA.
3. If politicians are able to extract resources from interest groups in exchange for the provision of particularized benefit without retribution from the public (see Olson, 1965; Grier and Munger, 1991), politicians will tend to do so, especially if the resource that is extracted can be used to retain office (Grier, Munger and Torrent, 1990). The emergence of such a relationship, however, may be detrimental to the creation of common or public goods by government because the aggregation of individual interests may not necessarily represent the common interest of society (Olson, 1965). Instead, the trade-offs associated with providing particularized benefits to special interests at a cost to the public good may induce strains on society and the economy.
4. It is at this point that interest groups, combined with the current system of campaign finance, create a rent-seeking outcome in congressional elections (Paul and Wilhite, 1990) and that incumbents demonstrate a substantial advantage over other candidates in raising money.

5. The activity of legislators under the existing campaign-finance system can be viewed as a political market in which special interests, acting as consumers, attempt to buy favorable policy from legislators (see Fiorina, 1989). Because the policy-provision market is constrained to relatively few legislators who can provide policy outputs, legislators are positioned to extract substantial resources from those interests (see Denzau and Munger, 1986; Tullock, 1980a, 1980b).

6. Members who are able to stay in office will be better positioned to extract substantial rents than do lame ducks or nonincumbents. The end of the stream of benefits derived by an interest from a retiring legislator is visible to the interest. What benefits the interest can obtain must be obtained quickly and at little long-term cost or must otherwise be insured as benefits after the legislator has left office (Parker, 1992a). Legislators who can produce benefits over a longer period of time are "investments," which interests can count on to provide and protect benefits for a longer period of time. Lame ducks are in the position to provide differential benefits, but their ability to do so is in the short term and does not constitute a potential longer-term relationship for the firms paying rents to legislators. Legislators' value drops as the time-horizon of their tenure draws short.

7. Rent seeking, in its most narrowly defined form, is the behavior of regulated firms attempting to obtain government monopolies from which they can extract extra profits in excess of their marginal costs of production. However, when we view the creation of policy or other goods in a market context, the concept of rent seeking can be extended to the behavior of legislators in the creation of policy. Indeed, Congress may represent one of the few self-regulated institutions in the United States.

2. Early money and profit taking in Senate campaigns

1. This is not to say that incumbents cannot influence policy once they leave office, for example, through lobbying. However, given the motivations of legislators to seek reelection, being inside the decision loop appears to be the preferred option.

2. Because a rent is an excess profit beyond the marginal cost of production and is acquired due to monopoly or oligopoly power in an exchange relationship, all financial contributions to incumbents can be considered rents because their membership in a legislative body automatically provides them such power.

3. The congressional election cycle is defined by House elections. Each House election ushers in a new Congress, with two thirds of incumbent Senators being retained from the previous Congress. Off-cycle years for a Senate class are those years in which a class of Senators is not up for reelection, and they constitute the first (early) and second (middle) Congresses in a Senator's six-year term.

4. Candidates may carry loans to their campaigns as debt to be repaid later, or likewise may obtain loans from banks or individuals not expecting immediate repayment. Incumbents therefore may not necessarily act to retire debt as quickly as they might to replenish cash stores, which they can personally control. There is also the possibility that loans may be forgiven without repayment, as Jay Rockefeller did with $12 million in loans to himself before his first reelection attempt.

5. Expenditures made in coordination with candidates, but spent by the national party on behalf of candidates, are permitted by section 441(d) of the Federal Election Campaign Act. The limits for party spending "on behalf" of candidates are higher than those for direct contributions to candidates and are adjusted for inflation.

6. From 1984 to 1990, the twenty most prolific rent gainers in the U.S. Senate retained $10.2 million in contributions beyond their reelection disbursements. The average rent retained was $196,038 in 1984; $304,995 in 1986; $286,910 in 1988; and $368,168 in 1990 (all monetary figures are expressed in constant 1990 dollars).
7. Interestingly enough, in their most recent campaigns for reelection, Phil Gramm with $727,615 in 1990 acquired substantial rents, whereas Fritz Hollings had a modest deficit of $2,052 in 1986.
8. For millionaires such as J. D. Rockefeller, Frank Lautenberg, Herb Kohl, and John Danforth, the need to externalize the costs of maintaining their seat may be lessened.

3. Targeting rent provisions by major interests

1. A composite index derived from the National Journal economic, social, and foreign policy scores offers a reasonable measure of incumbent ideology (see Smith, Herrerra, and Herrerra, 1990; and Poole, 1981). The scores are obtained from various issues of the National Journal.
2. Our measure of relative electoral marginality is defined as the remainder of 50 percent minus the incumbent Senator's total percentage of the two-party vote in the previous election.
3. For the purposes of testing these assumptions, we code marginality as the incumbent's share of the two-party vote in the last election subtracted from 50. For incumbents unopposed in their previous effort, the measure of marginality is −50. For an incumbent who won by a single vote, the marginality score is effectively 0. The direction of this coefficient is expected to be positive, with the benefit of a perfectly marginal incumbent being absorbed in the constant. Safer incumbents should have reduced receipts if the coefficient is positive. Marginality data were obtained from various issues of Barone and Ujifusa (1991).
4. To capture candidate political-quality effects, we employ a measure of challenger political quality that incorporates professional, celebrity, and elective and appointive political experience into one measure, with a maximum score of 8 (Green and Krasno, 1988). Candidates who have held prior elective office are initialized to 4. Candidates with elective experience have their score increased by +1 for each of the following attributes: incumbency in another office; holding high office (governor /Congress /Senate); prior run for this office (Senate); and celebrity status. Candidates who have not held prior office have their score initialized to 0, and can achieve a maximum score of 7. Their score increases by an additional +1 for being a party activist, having run for prior office, having run for high office (governor /Congress /Senate), prior Senate campaign, professional status, appointive political office, or celebrity status.
5. These data were provided by the Federal Elections Commission to the Inter-University Consortium for Political and Social Research. We gratefully acknowledge the provision of these data. Any errors in interpretation remain, of course, with the authors.
6. For Democrats, it is worth noting that a composite National Journal score of 40 or greater eradicates the detrimental impact of party on corporate receipts.
7. Because the direction of the ideology measures increasing liberalism as the index goes to 0, all effects of liberalism are captured in the constant.

4. Sitting in the cheap seats?

1. This chapter is not intended to be an encompassing examination of the dynamics of Senate elections. The most comprehensive treatment of Senate elections to date is Alan I. Abramowitz and Jeffrey A. Segal, *Senate Elections* (Ann Arbor: University of Michigan Press; 1992). We also suggest that the reader examine Mark C. Westlye, *Senate Elections and Campaign Intensity* (Baltimore: Johns Hopkins University Press; 1990); and James E. Campbell and Joe A. Sumners (1990), Presidential Coattails in Senate Elections, *American Political Science Review* 84: 513–24.
2. Election data are obtained from various editions of Michael Barone and Grant Ujifusa's *Almanac of American Politics* and Richard Scammons' *America Votes*.
3. The fact that incumbents are advantaged in spending is not surprising (see Jacobson, 1990; Jones, 1981).
4. Campaign-finance data are obtained from the Federal Elections Commission releases of campaign-finance reports through the ICPSR at the University of Michigan, FEC releases, and various issues of Barone and Ujifusa's *Almanac of American Politics*. All financial data are expressed in constant 1990 dollars, to control for inflationary effects on candidate expenditures.
5. If marginal returns are equal across all candidates, then the specification of a ratio is just as appropriate. However, we do not expect such a relationship to be in evidence. Candidate spending is coded with eight variables: Democratic Incumbent Spending, Republican Incumbent Spending, Democratic Challenger Spending, Republican Challenger Spending, and the quadratic of each of those variables. Where the specified candidate is not present in the case (i.e., no Democratic Challenger in a case where there is a Democratic Incumbent), the appropriate spending variable and its quadratic take on the value 0.
6. An impressive challenger profile is not always sufficient to create a competitive candidacy against an incumbent; exogenous issues and the quality of the campaign also affect the election outcome (see Patterson and Kephart, 1992). We acknowledge this, although in the vast number of cases experience does contribute to a challenger's competitiveness.
7. Initial regression analyses found that Republican and Democratic challengers obtained virtually identical benefits from experience. In our equation, we code challenger experience according to the Krasno and Green Index, and then multiply Republican challenger scores by -1 to account for the direction of experience effects.
8. Presidential coattails data are obtained from various editions of Barone and Ujifusa, *Almanac of American Politics*, and Scammons' *America Votes*.
9. Incumbency data are obtained from various editions of Barone and Ujifusa.
10. It is important to note that ordinary least squares (OLS) regression is not necessarily the best suited regression tool for estimating the impact of multiple independent variables on bounded independent variables. Ordinary least squares can generate estimated outcomes that fall beyond the range of possible outcomes (i.e., estimate vote percentages in excess of 100 percent or less than 0 percent). Tobit regression analysis is a preferable technique. However, Tobit and OLS techniques produced comparable results in our analysis. Given that OLS is an accepted tool of convention in most social sciences due to its ease of interpretability, we present the results of our OLS analyses.

11. Checks for multicollinearity were performed by examining the variance inflation factors of each independent variable. This examination reveals that there
is a relationship between the original and quadratic spending terms specified
for each candidate type. Likewise, the zero values for challenger spending
are negatively related to the variable values of incumbent spending. However, we are confident in the results of the equation. If the analysis is separated,
and Republican and Democratic incumbents are examined in isolation, the results are:

Variable	Republicans		Democrats	
	b	t	b	t
Constant	55.71		31.58	
Republican spending	3.27	1.68*	25.47	8.04***
Republican spending^2	−.17	−.42	−6.67	−5.85***
Democratic spending	−10.09	−5.84***	−9.79	−4.42***
Democratic spending^2	1.22	4.72***	1.74	4.25***
Presidential election year	−9.64	−1.32	−.24	−.04
Presidential coattails	.26	2.12**	.05	.43
Challenger political quality	−1.23	−3.68***	1.01	3.31***
Temporal control	.83	3.40***	−.09	−.34
Adjusted-R^2	.47		.46	
N	122		134	

* p < .010, two-tailed test; * p < .05, two-tailed test; *** p < .01, two-tailed test.

The relationship between incumbency and the Republican share of the vote is
extremely positive: Adjusted-R^2 = .43, constant = 47.13, b-coefficient of incumbency = 10.55, t-statistic = −14.13 (p < .0001). The separated analyses
indicate that the coefficients for spending in the combined analysis in Table 4.3
are virtually unchanged from the separate analyses by party. The inclusion of
the incumbency variable controls for an incumbency advantage that exists in-
dependently of spending. Although we acknowledge that there is multicollinearity present, the acceptance of the multicollinearity is necessary to
properly specify the spending-to-votes relationship.

12. Abramowitz and Segal (1992) estimate that the cost of running in California is
approximately 5.5 times that of running in Wyoming.

13. See the Keating Five example from the introduction.

5. Implications for campaign-finance reform

1. Business interests have been willing to work with Democrats and have gener-
ously rewarded Democratic incumbents who are ideologically receptive to the
entreaties of business interests (see Chapter 3). In addition, the Republican Party
enjoys less of an advantage in raising money than in 1980. The Democrats
steadily raised and contributed more money for their candidates throughout the

decade (see also Sorauf and Wilson, 1990). More recently, the Democrats nearly outstripped Republicans in total fund raising in 1992, and actually raised as much "soft" money as GOP committees.

2. A similar proposal enacted in Florida for state elections also limited PAC and soft-money contributions (Wetherell, 1991). The ensuing election produced noticeable gains in GOP representation in both legislative chambers. However, these gains might also be ascribed to redistricting.

6. Reform and rent-seeking legislature

1. Senators presently have a virtually unlimited horizon for fund raising from particularized interests. The six-year election cycle lends ample opportunity to raise sufficient funds for the next campaign, and many members use the entire cycle to fund war chests.

2. D'Amato's 1986 opponent, former Ralph Nadar associate Mark Green, pulls no punches in his assessment of the PAC system, especially when discussing D'Amato. In an interview with Abramowitz and Segal (1992: 172), Green stated that "accepting PAC money and then in effect arm-twisting government to enrich your PAC donors is unethical and should be illegal, and that's why I did ultimately file my ethics complaint against Senator D'Amato."

3. It also is worth noting that Deconcini's reelection prospects were problematic. He was censured for his role in the Keating Five scandal and trailed in early polls conducted in Arizona prior to announcing his retirement.

Bibliography

Abramowitz, A. I. 1980. A Comparison of Voting for U.S. Senator and Representative in 1978. *American Political Science Review* 74:633–40.

1988. Explaining Senate Election Outcomes. *American Political Science Review* 82:385–403.

1989. Campaign Spending in U.S. Senate Elections. *Legislative Studies Quarterly* 14:487–507.

Abramowitz, A. I., and J. P. Segal. 1992. *Senate Elections.* Ann Arbor: University of Michigan Press.

Alston, C. 1991a. Outlook for Law This Year Dim; Partisan Split Remains Wide. *Congressional Quarterly Weekly Report* 49 (May 18): 1,255–6.

1991b. Public Payments May Prove Achilles Heel on Floor. *Congressional Quarterly Weekly Report* 49 (November 16): 3,359–61.

Ansolabehere, S., R. Behr, and S. Iyengar. 1992. *The Media Game: American Politics in the Television Age.* New York: Macmillan.

Arrow, K. J. 1951. *Social Choice and Individual Values.* New York: John Wiley.

Barone, Michael, and Grant Ujifusa. 1991. *The Almanac of American Politics.* New York: Macmillan.

Becker, G. 1983. A Theory of Competition Among Pressure Groups for Political Influence. *Quarterly Journal of Economics* 98:371–400.

Bernstein, R. A. 1989. *Elections, Representation, and Congressional Voting Behavior.* Englewood Cliffs, NJ: Prentice-Hall.

Berry, J. 1984. *The Interest Group Society.* Boston: Little, Brown.

Brace, P. 1984. Progressive Ambition in the House: A Probabilistic Approach. *Journal of Politics* 46: 556–71.

Buchanan, J. M. 1980. Rent Seeking and Profit Seeking. In J. M. Buchanan, R. D. Tollison, and G. Tullock, eds., *Toward a Theory of the Rent-Seeking Society.* College Station: Texas A&M Press.

Bullock III, C. S. 1988. Regional Realignment From an Officeholding Perspective. *Journal of Politics* 50:553–74.

Calhoun, J. C. 1954. Disquisition on Government. In D. Katz, ed., *Public Opinion and Propaganda.* New York: The Dryden Press.

Campbell, J. E. 1993. Divided Government, Partisan Bias and Turnout in Congressional Elections: Do Democrats Sit in the 'Cheap Seats?' Paper originally presented at the 1991 annual meeting of the American Political Science Association, Washington, DC.

Campbell, J. E., and J. A. Sumners. 1990. Presidential Coattails in Senate Elections. *American Political Science Review* 84:513–24.

Campbell, J. E., J. R. Alford, and K. Henry. 1984. Television Markets and Congressional Elections. *Legislative Studies Quarterly* 9: 665–78.

Cantor, J. E. 1986. *Campaign Financing in the Federal Elections: A Guide to the Law and Its Operation.* CRS Report for Congress 91–770 GOV.

———. 1993. *Campaign Financing.* CRS Report for Congress IBS7020.

Cantor, J. E., and D. C. Huckabee. 1993. *Senate Campaign Expenditures, Receipts and Sources of Funds: 1980–92.* CRS Report for Congress.

Caro, R. A. 1982. *The Years of Lyndon Johnson.* New York: Knopf.

Chubb, J. E. 1988. Institutions, the Economy, and the Dynamics of State Elections. *American Political Science Review* 82:133–54.

Comark Enterprises. 1992. *Television and Cable Factbook.* Colmar, PA: Comark Enterprises.

Congressional Quarterly Special Reports: Elections (1972–92, inclusive). Washington, DC: CQ Press.

Denzau, A. T., and M. C. Munger 1986. Legislators and Interest Groups: How Unorganized Interests Get Represented. *American Political Science Review* 80:89–106.

Dewar, H. 1991. Trouble Fielding a Team: For Want of Candidates, the GOP Could Lose Big in '92. *Washington Post Weekly Edition* (August 19–25): 12.

Downs, A. 1957. *An Economic Theory of Democracy.* New York: Harper & Row.

Ehrenhalt, A. 1991. *The United States of Ambition.* New York: Times Books.

Eismeier, T. J., and P. H. Pollock III. 1986a. Strategy and Choice in Congressional Elections: The Role of Political Action Committees. *American Journal of Political Science* 30:197–213.

———. 1986b. Politics and Markets: Corporate Money in American National Elections. *British Journal of Political Science* 16:287–309.

Enelow, J. M. and M. J. Hitnich. 1984. *The Spatial Theory of Voting.* Cambridge: Cambridge University Press.

Etzioni, A. 1990. *Capitol Corruption.* New York: Macmillan.

Evans, D. 1988. Oil PACs and Aggressive Contribution Strategies. *Journal of Politics* 50:1,047–56.

Fenno, R. F. 1978: *Homestyle.* Boston: Little, Brown.

———. 1982. *The United States Senate: A Bicameral Perspective.* Washington, DC: American Enterprise Institute.

———. 1989. *The Making of A Senator: Dan Quayle.* Washington, DC: CQ Press.

———. 1991a. *When Incumbency Fails: The Senate Career of Mark Andrews.* Washington, DC: CQ Press.

———. 1991b. *Learning to Legislate: The Senate Education of Arlen Specter.* Washington, DC: CQ Press.

Ferejohn, J. A. 1977. On the Decline of Competition in Congressional Elections. *American Political Science Review* 71:166–76.

Fiorina, M. P. 1989. *Congress: Keystone of the Washington Establishment.* New Haven, CT: Yale University Press.

Fritz, S., and D. Morris. 1992. *Gold–Plated Politics: Running for Congress in the 1990s.* Washington, DC: CQ Press.

Glantz, S. A., A. I. Abramowitz, and M. P. Burkart. 1976. Election Outcomes: Whose Money Matters? *Journal of Politics* 38:1,033–8.

Godwin, R. K. 1988. *One Billion Dollars of Influence.* Chatham, NJ: Chatham House.

Gopoian, D. 1984. What Makes PACs Tick? An Analysis of the Allocation Patterns of Economic Interest Groups. *American Journal of Political Science* 28: 259–81.

Green, D. P., and J. S. Krasno. 1988. Salvation for the Spendthrift Incumbent: Reestimating the Effects of Campaign Spending in House Elections. *American Journal of Political Science* 32: 884–907.

Grier, K. B. 1989. Campaign Spending and Senate Elections, 1978–1984. *Public Choice* 63:201–19.

Grier, K. B., and M. C. Munger. 1986. The Impact of Legislator Attributes on Interest Group Campaign Contributions. *Journal of Labor Research* 7:349–61.

———. 1991. Committee Assignments, Constituent Preferences, and Campaign Contributions. *Economic Inquiry* 29:24–43.

———. 1993. Comparing Interest Group PAC Contributions to House and Senate Incumbents, 1980–1986. *Journal of Politics* 55:615–43.

Grier, K. B., M. C. Munger, and G. M. Torrent. 1990. Allocation Patterns of PAC Monies: The U.S. Senate. *Public Choice* 67:111–28.

Harris, A., and S. M. Milkis. 1989. *The Politics of Regulatory Change.* New York: Oxford University Press.

Herrnson, P. 1989. National Party Decision Making, Strategies, and Resource Distribution in Congressional Elections. *Western Political Quarterly* 42: 301–23.

Jacobson, G. C. 1975. The Impact of Broadcast Campaigning on Electoral Outcomes. *Journal of Politics* 37:769–93.

———. 1976. Practical Consequences of Campaign Finance Reform: An Incumbency Protection Act? *Public Policy* 24:1–32.

———. 1978. The Effects of Campaign Spending in Congressional Elections. *American Political Science Review* 72:769–83.

———. 1985. Money and Votes Reconsidered: Congressional Elections, 1972–1982. *Public Choice* 47:7–62.

———. 1989. Parties and PACs in Congressional Elections. In L. C. Dodd and B. I. Oppenheimer, eds., *Congress Reconsidered.* 4th ed. Washington, DC: CQ Press.

———. 1990. *The Electoral Origins of Divided Government: Competition in U.S. House Elections, 1946–1988.* Boulder, CO: Westview Press.

———. 1992. *The Politics of Congressional Election.* 3d ed. New York: HarperCollins.

Jacobson, G. L., and S. Kernell. 1983. *Strategy and Choice in Congressional Elections.* 2d ed. New Haven, CT: Yale University Press.

Jones, C. O. 1981. New Directions in U.S. Congressional Research. *Legislative Studies Quarterly* 6:458.

Keech, W. R. 1991. Politics, Economics, and Politics Again. *Journal of Politics* 53: 597–611.

Kingdon, J. W. 1984. *Agendas, Alternatives, and Public Policies.* Boston: Little, Brown.

Kostroski, W. L. 1973. Party and Incumbency in Postwar Senate Elections: Trends, Patterns, and Models. *American Political Science Review* 67:1,213–34.

Krasno, J. S., and D. P. Green. 1988. Preempting Quality Challengers in House Elections. *Journal of Politics,* 50:920–36.

Locke, J. 1980. *Two Treatises of Government.* In C. B. Macpherson, introductory editor, *John Locke: The Second Treatise of Government.* Indianapolis: Hackett.

Lott, J. R. 1990. Attendance Rates, Political Shirking, and the Effect of Post Elective Office Employment. *Economic Inquiry* 28:133–50.

Madison, J. A. [1787] 1969. *Notes of Debates in the Federal Convention of 1787.* New York: Norton.

Malbin, M. J. 1980. *Unelected Representatives: Congressional Staff and the Future of Representative Government.* New York: Basic.

Matthews, D. E. 1960. *U.S. Senators and Their World.* New York: Random House.

Mayhew, D. R. 1974. *Congress: The Electoral Connection.* New Haven, CT: Yale University Press.

McCubbins, M. 1985. The Legislative Design of Regulatory Structure. *American Journal of Political Science* 29:721–38.

McCubbins, M., and T. Page. 1985. The Congressional Foundations of Agency Performance. *Public Choice* 51:173–90.

Miller, M. 1980. *Lyndon: An Oral Biography*. New York: Putnam.

Mitchell, W. C., and M. C. Munger. 1991. Economic Models of Interest Groups: An Introductory Survey. *American Journal of Political Science* 35:512–46.

Munger, M. C. 1989. A Simple Test of the Thesis That Committee Jurisdictions Shape Corporate PAC Contributions. *Public Choice* 62:181–6.

Nagler, J., and J. Leighley. 1992. Presidential Campaign Expenditures: Evidence on Allocations and Effects. *Public Choice* 73:319–33.

Olson, M. 1965. *The Logic of Collective Action*. Cambridge: Harvard University Press.

Ornstein, N. J., T. E. Mann, and M. J. Malbin. 1991. *Vital Statistics on Congress, 1991–1992*. Washington, DC: CQ Press.

Parker, G. R. 1992a. The Distribution of Honoraria Income in the U.S. Congress: Who Gets Rents in Legislatures and Why? *Public Choice* 73:167–81.

1992b. *Institutional Change, Discretion, and the Making of Modern Congress: An Economic Interpretation*. Ann Arbor: University of Michigan Press.

Parker, G. R., and S. L. Parker. 1979. Factions in Committees: The U. S. House of Representatives. *American Political Science Review* 78:64–76.

Patterson, S. C., and T. W. Kephart. 1992. The Case of the Wayfaring Challenger: The 1988 Senate Election in Ohio. *Congress and the Presidency*, 18:105–20.

Paul, C., and A. Wilhite. 1990. Efficient Rent-Seeking Under Varying Cost Structures. *Public Choice* 64:279–90.

Pindyck, R.S., and D. C. Rubinfeld. 1981. *Econometric Models and Economic Forecasts*. 2d ed. New York: McGraw Hill.

Poole, K. T. 1981. Dimensions of Interest Group Evaluation of the U.S. Senate, 1969–1980. *American Journal of Political Science* 25:49–67.

Poole, K. T. and T. Romer. 1985. Patterns of Political Action Committee Contributions to the 1980 Campaigns for the United States House of Representatives. *Public Choice* 47:63–111.

Poole, K. T., T. Romer, and H. Rosenthal. 1987. The Revealed Preferences of Political Action Committees. *American Economic Review* 77:298–302.

Posner, R. A. 1974. Theories of Economic Regulation. *Bell Journal of Economics and Management Science* 5: 335–58.

Regens, J. L. 1989. Congressional Cosponsorship of Acid Rain Controls. *Social Science Quarterly* 70:505–12.

Regens, J. L., and E. Elliott. 1992. Political and Economic Influences on Private-Sector Pollution Control Costs. *Western Political Quarterly* 45:113–24.

Regens, J. L., E. Elliott, and R. K. Gaddie. 1991. Regulatory Costs, Committee Jurisdictions, and Corporate PAC Contributions. *Social Science Quarterly* 72:751–60.

Regens, J. L., R. K. Gaddie, and E. Elliott. 1993. Member Attributes and Corporate Contributions to U.S. Senators: Do Environmental Compliance Costs Matter? *Canadian Journal of Political Science* 19:331–42.

1994. Corporate Campaign Contributions and Rent Provision in Senate Elections. *Social Science Quarterly* 75:152–65.

Rohde, D. 1979. Risk-Bearing and Progressive Ambition: The Case of Members of the United States House of Representatives. *American Journal of Political Science* 23:1–26.

Sabato, L. J. 1985. *PAC Power: Inside the World of Political Action Committees*. New York: Norton.

Salisbury, R. H. 1984. Interest Representation: The Dominance of Institutions. *American Political Science Review* 77:64–76.

Silberman, J., and G. Yochum. 1978. The Role of Money in Determining Election Outcomes. *Social Science Quarterly* 58:671–82.

Sinclair, B. 1988. The Distribution of Committee Positions in the U.S. Senate: Explaining Institutional Change. *American Journal of Political Science* 32:276–301.

———. 1989. *The Transformation of the U.S. Senate*. Baltimore: Johns Hopkins University Press.

Smith, E. R. A. N., R. Herrerra, and C. L. Herrerra. 1990. The Measurement Characteristics of Congressional Roll-Call Indexes. *Legislative Studies Quarterly* 15:283–95.

Smith, F. E. 1964. *Congressman from Mississippi*. New York: Pantheon.

Sorauf, F. J. 1988. *Money in American Elections*. Glenview, IL: Scott, Foresman.

Sorauf, F. J., and S. A. Wilson. 1990. Campaigns and Money: A Changing Role for the Parties? In L. S. Maisel, ed., *The Parties Respond: Changes in the American Party System*. Boulder, CO: Westview Press.

Squire, P. 1989. Challengers in U.S. Senate Elections. *Legislative Studies Quarterly* 14:531–47.

———. 1991. Preemptive Fund-raising and Challenger Profile in Senate Elections. *Journal of Politics* 53: 1,150–64.

Stanley, H. W., and R. G. Niemi. 1992. *Vital Statistics on American Politics*. Washington, DC: CQ Press.

Stigler, G. J. 1971. The Theory of Economic Regulation. *Bell Journal of Economics and Management Science* 2:137–46.

———. 1987. *The Theory of Price*. 4th ed. New York: Macmillan.

Sundquist, J. L. 1968. *Politics and Policy: The Eisenhower, Kennedy, and Johnson Years*. Washington, DC: Brookings Institution.

Thomas, S. J. 1989. Do Incumbent Campaign Expenditures Matter? *Journal of Politics* 51:965–76.

Tollison, R. D. 1982. Rent Seeking: A Survey. *Kyklos* 35:575–602.

Tullock, G. 1965. *The Politics of Bureaucracy*. Washington, DC: Public Affairs Press.

———. 1980a. The Welfare Costs of Tariffs, Monopolies, and Theft. In J. M. Buchanan, R. D. Tollison, and G. Tullock, eds., *Toward a Theory of the Rent Seeking Society*. College Station: Texas A&M Press.

———. 1980b. Efficient Rent Seeking. In J. M. Buchanan, R. Tollison, and G. Tullock, eds., *Toward a Theory of the Rent Seeking Society*. College Station: Texas A&M Press.

Wartzman, R. 1994. Defending Football and Fancy Cars, Politicians Decry Effort to Limit Use of Campaign Money. *The Wall Street Journal* 223 (January 12): A12.

Westlye, M. C. 1991. *Senate Elections and Campaign Intensity*. Baltimore: Johns Hopkins University Press.

Wetherell, T. K. 1991. Florida Takes the Big Money out of Political Campaigns. *State Legislatures* (August): 44.

White, T. H. 1976. *Breach of Faith*. New York: Atheneum.

Wilhite, A., and C. Paul. 1989. Corporate Campaign Contributions and Legislative Voting. *Quarterly Review of Economics and Business* 29:73–85.

Wood, B. D. 1988. Principals, Bureaucrats, and Responsiveness in Clean Air Enforcements. *American Political Science Review* 82:213–45.

———. 1990. Does Politics Make a Difference at the EEOC? *American Journal of Political Science* 24:503–30.

Wright, J. R. 1989. PAC Contributions, Lobbying, and Representation. *Journal of Politics* 51:713–29.

INDEX

117

118   Index